CrazyBusy

CrazyBusy

Overstretched, Overbooked, and About to Snap!
Strategies for Handling Your Fast-Paced Life

\\

Edward M. Hallowell, M.D.

BALLANTINE BOOKS

NEW YORK

2007 Ballantine Books Trade Paperback Edition

Copyright © 2006 by Edward M. Hallowell, M.D.

All rights reserved.

Published in the United States by Ballantine Books, an imprint of The Random House Publishing Group, a division of Random House, Inc., New York.

BALLANTINE and colophon are registered trademarks of Random House, Inc.

Originally published in hardcover in the United States by Ballantine Books, an imprint of The Random House Publishing Group, a division of Random House, Inc., in 2006.

Grateful acknowledgement is made to the following for permission to reprint previously published materials:

Families and Work Institute: Excerpt from the study "Overwork in America: When the Way We Work Becomes Too Much" from Families and Work Institute, March 15, 2005 (http://familiesandwork.org). Reprinted by permission of Families and Work Institute.

Garp Enterprises, Ltd.: Excerpt from an essay by John Irving published in *Transitions: Exeter Remembered 1961–1987* (Phillips Exeter Academy, 1990). Reprinted by permission of Garp Enterprises, Ltd.

Reprint Management Services: Excerpt from "Bored on the Phone? Beware of the Jerk-o-meter" by Michael Kunzelman, copyright © 2005 by The Associated Press (The Associated Press, August 11, 2005). All rights reserved. Reprinted by permission of Reprint Management Services on behalf of The Associated Press.

Solo Syndication: Excerpt from "Tired women suffer phone text stress" by Alexa Baracaia, copyright © 2005 by Associated Newspapers Ltd. (The Evening Standard, London, January 6, 2005). Reprinted by permission of *The Evening Standard*. Rights administered by Solo Syndication.

LIBRARY OF CONGRESS CATALOGING-IN-PUBLICATION DATA
Hallowell, Edward M.
    CrazyBusy : overstretched, overbooked, and about to snap : strategies for coping in a world gone ADD / Edward M. Hallowell.
        p. cm.
    ISBN 978-0-345-48244-0
    1. Conduct of life. I. Title.
    BF637.C5H296 2006
    158—dc22   2005057088

Printed in the United States of America

www.ballantinebooks.com

9 8

For my dear friend and agent, Jill Kneerim, upon whose face
I always see smiles and in whose voice I always
hear laughter and feel warmth

And, as always, for Sue, Lucy, Jack, and Tucker
I love you soooooooooooooooooooooooooooo much.

Contents

\\

Part One
Overbooked and About to Snap

Part Two
Creating a System That Works for You

\\\

Overbooked
and About to Snap

1

The Peculiar Life We Lead, or, The Agony of a Rotary Phone

My family stayed at a lakeside cottage last summer where the only telephone was an old-fashioned rotary model. The cottage was so remote that there was no cell phone service, just the stolid black telephone sitting atop a tattered phone book on an end table next to a worn-out peach-colored couch.

I remember the first time I dialed that phone. It was morning. I'd gone out for a wake-me-up swim, poured myself a cup of coffee, and was sitting on the couch to call a friend to see if he and his kids might like to join my wife, my kids, and me that night at a minor league baseball game. There was no urgency to this call, no need for me to hurry.

Yet as I started to dial, I got angry, and impatience flamed within me because on this phone I had to wait for the rotor to wind back to its starting point after each number. It was so slow! In addition, it made an irritating screeching sound as it retraced its cycle, like a rusty metal drawer stuck on its runners: 5 . . . 4 . . . 2 . . . 6 . . . I could have entered the entire number on a touch-tone phone in the time it took me to dial just **one** number on this obsolete contraption. Not to mention how much faster I could have done it with speed dial had I been able to use my cell phone.

By the time I had laboriously cranked out the entire number, I was in a total snit. How could anyone still own such a slow phone? I fumed. What a stupid phone! How backward! How dumb! But then I caught myself. This was absurd. When my friend finally answered, I spoke to him, hung up, and then redialed his number, timing how long it took me: eleven seconds exactly. As if putting my life in danger, those eleven slow seconds had annoyed me beyond reason. What a fool I had become. What a modern man. I felt embarrassed at my automatic impatience. I had become a man in a hurry even when I had no need to hurry.

As the vacation moved along, I changed. I made friends with that old rotary phone. I began to appreciate what it could teach me. The sound it made started to sound less like a stuck drawer and more like an old windmill still stoutly doing its work after all these years. I came to think of it as a wise counsel, ensconced on its end table like a Buddha cautioning me to take my time and enjoy, while they lasted, the summer, the childhood of my kids, the ripening of my marriage, and these best years of my life.

Without intending for it to happen or knowing how it got started, many people now find that they live in a rush they don't want and didn't create, or at least didn't mean to create. If you feel busier now than you've ever been before, and if you wonder if you can keep up this pace much longer, don't feel alone. Most of us feel slightly bewildered, realizing we have more to do than ever—with less time to do it.

Look at what's happened to the usual "how are you" exchange. It used to go like this: "How are you?" "Fine." Now it often goes like this: "How are you?" "Busy." Or, "Too busy." Or even, "Crazy busy."

If you're busy doing what matters to you, then being busy is bliss. You've found a rhythm for your life that works for you. This world is bursting with possibilities; its energy can be contagious. If you catch the bug, you want to jump out of bed each day and get busy, not because you are run ragged by details or because you are keeping the wolf from your door, but because you are in love with this fast life. At its best, modern life dazzles us, giving us a chance to get more done in a minute than used to get done in a month.

But if being busy keeps you from doing what matters most to you, or if it leads you to do things you deem unwise, like getting angry at a rotary telephone, then being busy is a problem. This book is about both the problem and the opportunity—where this peculiar life comes from and how to turn it to your advantage.

In order to make this crazy world work for you and not against you, you must decide what matters to you most and focus your attention on that. In days gone by, this was not nearly as difficult as it is today. That's because the selection was not nearly as broad, and the thieves of time, attention, and mental energy were not nearly as common or as clever as they are today. Today, these thieves have never had it so good. If you're not wise to their tricks, it is likely that they will run you faster and faster as they steal more and more of your time, attention, and energy, leaving you less and less for what you want to do.

Being too busy, which can seem necessary and unavoidable, can become a habit so entrenched that it leads you to postpone or cut short what really matters to you, making you a slave to a lifestyle you don't like but can't escape. You can be so busy that you don't even take the time to decide what actually does matter most to you, let alone make the time to do it.

Others created this lifestyle. It looked like the only way to go, the way of the future. What were you supposed to do, be a Luddite and refuse to buy a cell phone or a BlackBerry? Not go wireless? Refuse to enroll your kids in soccer, violin, and SAT tutoring? Refuse to take on the added debt of the extra week of vacation your spouse and kids were counting on? Have simple birthday parties the way they used to in the 1950s and 1960s? Figure out a way to live with just one car? Or just two? Say no to braces for your daughter? Let your yard go to seed? Refuse to give your time to the cancer foundation your friend is heading up? Refuse to do the extra work your boss asks you to do because half your staff got laid off? What if you're next?

Unaware of the hidden consequences, and without making a conscious decision to do so, soon you found that you and your family had joined right in. It happened slowly, over the past five to ten years. Had you known then what you know now, you might have done things differently. It is like the story of frogs in water. If you put a frog in a pot of boiling water, he will try to jump out. But if you put a frog in a pot of cold water and heat it up slowly, you will end up with a boiled frog.

Someone turned up the burner on us in the mid-1990s. We're not boiled yet, but we're definitely feeling the heat. Before the water boils, it might be a good idea to jump out. Not jump out of modern life and head off to Walden Pond (though even *it* swarms with busy tourists), but adjust the temperature yourself instead of letting some diabolical chef set it for you.

The greatest damage from being too busy is that it prevents people from setting their own temperature, controlling their own lives. It does other harm as well, like increasing toxic stress, making people sick, causing accidents and errors, turning otherwise polite people rude, and reducing the general level of happiness in the population. But the greatest damage it does is that it keeps a person from what's most important.

Being too busy is a persistent and pestering problem, one that is leading tens of millions of Americans to feel as if they were living in a swarm of gnats constantly taking bites out of their lives. All the screaming and swatting in the world does not make them go away. Being too busy plagues the best and brightest people in this country, if not the world. Legions of smart people everywhere feel overly busy; they rack their brains to find a better way, struggling to regain control of their lives. I want to explore this difficult problem, offer some solutions that can work for you, and most important, prompt you to create your own solutions.

2 This Attention Deficit World: Frantic, Free, and Out of Control

Swirling around, swept into the air like dry leaves before a great storm, we're tossed about by forces we invented but no longer control. The wind rules, picking us up and taking us where it blows.

Busy. Fast. Wired. Going who knows where. Welcome to our attention deficit world.

In its energy, excitement, and excess, in its novelty, speed, chaos, and confusion, in its dust storm of data, in its creative spirit and freedom from convention, in its emphasis on adaptability and on the *now*, in its ever changing nature, in its irreverence and incoherence, today's world looks much like another world I know well: the world of attention deficit disorder, or ADD.

ADD is a medical condition I have specialized in diagnosing and treating for the past twenty-five years. I have come to see it as a metaphor for modern life, offering a model—as well as a guide—for what's happening today in a world where we are living a kind of life never lived before. Once applicable only to a relative few, the symptoms of ADD now seem to describe just about everybody.

People with untreated ADD rush around a lot, feel impatient wherever they are, love speed, get frustrated easily, lose focus in the middle of a task or a conversation because some other thought catches their attention, bubble with energy but struggle to pay attention to one issue for more than a few seconds, talk fast or feel at a loss for words, often forget where they're going or what they're going to get, have bright ideas but can't implement them, fail to complete what they're doing, have many projects going simultaneously but chronically postpone completing them, make decisions impulsively because their brain's circuitry is overloaded, feel they could do a lot more if they could just get it together, get angry easily when interrupted, feel powerless over the piles of *stuff* that surround them, resolve each day to do better tomorrow, and in general feel busy beyond belief but not all that productive.

Many people who *do not* have true ADD *do have* many of those symptoms these days. You might say they suffer from a severe case of modern life.

The practical lessons I have learned from working in the world of ADD can be generalized into lessons about how to handle modern life. Many skills and techniques people use to manage ADD apply to today's busy world, helping a person take advantage of its opportunities while avoiding its peculiar new dangers. While living life today can seem like riding a bike no-handed while reading a book and juggling six eggs, it doesn't have to be like that.

How many people feel too rushed to do what matters most to them? How many people feel in a hurry all day and into the night? How many people can't take the time to stop and think? People are trying to recapture their hold on life, to take back the time that's mysteriously been stolen from them, and to regain the control they've unintentionally given away.

Paradoxically enough, it is in part the desire for control that has led people to lose it. Paradoxes abound in our busy new world. The control paradox is but one. By trying to control life as much as possible, you can run yourself ragged, *losing* control in the process. You can feel like a tin can surrounded by a circle of a hundred powerful magnets. Pulled at once in every direction, you go nowhere but instead spin faster and faster on your axis.

In part, many people are excessively busy because they allow themselves to respond to every magnet: tracking too much data, processing too much information, answering to too many people, taking on too many tasks—all out of a sense that this is the way they *must* live in order to keep up and stay in control. But it's the magnets that have the control. We have magnetized our electronic devices (to use the airlines' term), our material possessions, our children's grades and even toys, our career goals, the laundry, the dentist appointment, the up-to-the-second news and expert advice, and even our vacations to such an extent that we have all but given away our free time, our time to do nothing but breathe in, breathe out, and feel the earth beneath our feet. We could take a lesson from that old rotary phone—not to bring back the good old days, but to keep the current days from stealing from us what's good.

Modern life makes us feel as if we can be everywhere and do everything, and it gives us magical tools that heighten that illusion. Only when we accept that we *can't* track and control every variable do we finally give up trying. Then we can demagnetize the magnets surrounding us. The tin can can stop spinning.

When we stop responding to everyone and everything, we regain the control we can effectively exert. We give up pursuing total control and better use what we have. We learn the wisdom of what a rabbi once said: "Happiness is not having what you want but wanting what you have." We control enough of life to relish what we have. Then we gain dependable joy. As Samuel Johnson said some 250 years ago, "The pleasures of sudden wonder are soon exhausted, and the mind can only repose upon the stability of truth." Paradoxically, at the core of that "stability" is the acceptance of instability, of change.

This is not the wisdom of just an anonymous rabbi or an eighteenth-century essayist. It is also practical street smarts, the wisdom of, say, the veteran stock picker. Great investors like Warren Buffett don't follow each stock they own minute to minute, day to day, or even week to week. They make their picks, then let go of control. They wait a few years and let the stock do the work. They give control to the company they felt good enough about to invest in in the first place. And they are never too busy to think.

Of course, many practical concerns keep people busy, but behind all of them lies a reason most people don't acknowledge or even perceive. At the deepest level—the level we rarely visit—we stay busy to *avoid* looking into the abyss.

Now and then we have to—someone dies too young, a bad guy wins, or a hurricane hits—but most of the time we manage to avert our gaze from all that. We keep busy to warm us with feelings of power, productivity, and progress. We feed the illusion that we can defeat death, that ultimate confounder of our control. We stay busy to look away from loss, tragedy, and pain. We stay busy to control the whole shebang.

Of course, death wins. All the activity the whole world can generate can't bring back one person who has died. This is perhaps the hardest truth any of us ever learns. Acceptance—not busyness—brings us to a peaceful place. By accepting that we do not have total control, by accepting death, by accepting our place in nature, we gain the fullest life and what control we are meant to have.

3 The Rush, the Gush, the Worry, and the Blather

Four qualities color today's life with its peculiar attention-stealing hues: the *rush*, the *gush*, the *worry*, and the *blather* (which also includes *clutter*). Each can be distracting as well as riveting. Combined, they can steal your attention and wear you out.

By the rush, I refer to the turbocharged speed of life today. Have you ever sent a handwritten letter, or gotten out of your chair to change the station on your TV, or taken the train for a trip of more than two hundred miles? Have you ever cashed a check with a bank teller? Have you ever used a typewriter? Do you have ice trays in your freezer? Have you ever cranked down the window in a car? When was the last time you used a pay phone? For most people, all of that is in the slow, slow past.

By the gush, I mean the volume of data that pelts our brains like sleet that won't melt, sleet we must catch, organize, make sense of, and respond to each day. Have you ever counted up the number of messages you get and send in a day, including e-mail, voice mail, and messages others take for you or that you leave? Have you ever contemplated the number of bits of information you *could* gain access to every time you log on? Have you ever considered how many bits of data you actually do carry in your conscious brain in comparison with how many you believe you should or others expect you to?

We all know the meaning of the third quality of modern life I single out—namely, worry. What makes worry peculiar these days is how common it is, even among children, and how toxic it can be, leading many people to hold back on life out of fear. Furthermore, worry and anxiety, which are epidemic in today's world, in and of themselves reduce mental focus and create a distracted state that can look like real ADD.

By blather and its sibling clutter, I refer to the colossal, growing mess of words, images, numbers, noises, and physical objects that roll over us every day like the Blob from the 1950s horror movie. This stuff oozes out of televisions, radios, magazines, billboards, books, mail, and other printed material and congeals in the piles we put it all into, along with the other junk modern life upchucks like mountains of used tires. The piles tumble down around our work and living spaces and ominously remain, waiting for the signal to organize and unite into one gigantic Megablob the size of the earth, protruding like a horrific tumor so big that it will set the world off its orbit.

To oppose the Blob, you have to be much more selective than people have ever had to be. Decide what matters and do it. Regulate the rush, the gush, and the rest, or they will regulate you. Hard as it is to believe, each is actually a potential ally if you use them all in the service of accomplishing what matters. The rush can be the convenience and efficiency that speed provides. The gush can be the cyberlibrary we all can gain entrance to, even from home, a library that dwarfs all others. Worry used properly is an adaptive warning signal, a mental advantage given us by our ability both to recollect and to anticipate. Unlike toxic worry, wise worry is a key to success. Finally, the blather and the clutter become allies when we learn how to keep them at bay, extracting from the mess only what we need.

But who has time to make a plan to turn these forces into the allies they might be? You're much more likely to wing it, right? Time presses us so relentlessly that winging it seems to be the only possible strategy. We get up each day and wing it, building today upon the undone remnants of yesterday, coupled with the anticipated as well as unanticipated demands of today.

A plan could help, if formulated in the right way. What I offer is not a plan rooted in the detailed, insufferably boring, imagination-deadening sense of that word, but a plan that's more like signs along the road. Turn left for Boston, right for New York. Go sixty-five if you don't want to risk getting a ticket. If you don't care, go as fast as you like, but bear in mind you're risking your life and the lives of others. Stop here if you want to avoid having an accident. You can ignore all the signs if you want; you retain control. Therefore, you can use your initiative and creativity at will. You make your own route. I am simply offering you the benefit of my experience and those of others in navigating this unpredictable ADD-like world.

4 Amid a Sea of Uncertainty

Our peculiar times seem to be leading up to some epochal phase change, comparable to what happens to physical bodies when they reach a certain temperature or speed. How fast can we go, how busy can we get before we fundamentally change? Wherever we're headed, we're headed there fast.

We've heard predictions, most of which we ignore because we don't know what else to do with them. Whether it's economic distress due to global competition and our own overspending, or physical distress due to global warming and our own misuse of the planet, or pandemic illness due to a resistant virus, or political distress due to global power shifts and our own misuse of power, we are aware of the dangers that might soon cataclysmically change our lives for the worse.

On the other hand, life today is good in so many ways that we feel grateful even as we worry. It makes me think of how I feel toward the end of a great party where I've had an especially wonderful time. I wish I could make the party last forever, but I know tomorrow will come, and I know what to expect in the letdown. But as *this* party moves toward its farewells, nobody knows what tomorrow will bring.

Life today teeters on a pinnacle surrounded by a sea of uncertainty. And so it did well before 9/11 and Hurricane Katrina. Yet, buoyed by perhaps unreasonable optimism, we work harder than ever, trying to hold on to what we have and to make it better. You don't see many people giving up. Just the opposite. Most people are working as hard as they can. Through hard work coupled with cockeyed optimism and smart decisions, we rise to the peculiar challenges of life today.

But the challenges are peculiar and daunting, more so than most of us realize. For example, how much do you really know about global warming? I didn't know much, but because I wanted to get an expert's view on an important issue I didn't understand in order to show how busyness can keep a person (me) from keeping up with issues that really matter, I called Jim Anderson, professor of chemistry at Harvard and one of the world's experts on climate. He told me he was "not sanguine" (that's professorese for scared as hell), having looked at the latest data showing how much of the polar ice cap had already melted. As he went into the gory details, the part of my mind that can no longer hear about Big Problems I Can't Solve went numb. And global warming is just *one* of the many challenges we face. AIDS. Resistant bacteria and viruses. Deforestation. A national debt like we've never had before, plus an emerging China holding so many of our notes. The unexplained rise in asthma, autism, allergies, and Asperger's syndrome. Terrorism.

The subject of this book, the puzzling fact of how extraordinarily *busy* so many of us have become, is more mundane than the Big Problems, but worth writing about in part because it keeps many of us from understanding the Big Problems. It also hits most of us closer to home right now than the Big Problems do. Right now we need a chart just to get through traffic.

And how uncharted this uncertain world is, both at the macro level (Big Problems) and the micro (traffic, lost socks, which vitamins to take). Bursting with energy, busy beyond belief, fast and full of dangers never imagined—let alone encountered—until now, but also full of new opportunities and excitement instigated by instant access to everyone and everything all the time, today's world is an international, multilingual, multimodal carnival evolving unstoppably, threatening to leave millions behind but also offering the chance for millions of others to jump on and lead the way for the first time. The old charts, like so much of what we used to count on, are disappearing.

From physics to friendships, from cosmology to cameras and computers, from what we do and what our children do to how we keep track of what we do and how others keep track of us, from what your employer can promise you to the lifestyle you can expect, everywhere you look, what was familiar has changed. No one knows what will be, what to hold on to, and what to reject.

While politicians and policy makers offer simplistic solutions to calm our nerves and quiet us down, the wise among us know that this world is so complex and unpredictable that simplistic solutions will leave people lost, disappointed, and ill equipped to thrive in tomorrow's world, like people who can memorize but who can't think.

The wise will be humble enough to listen to others, creative enough to devise new solutions to our new problems, and bold enough in the face of uncertainty to give them a try.

5 The Myth and Reality of Multitasking

"Multitasking" refers to a mythical activity in which people believe they can perform two or more tasks simultaneously as effectively as one. To appreciate how faulty this notion is, consider how you behave in your car when you get lost. As you focus and try to get your bearings, one of the first things you do is turn down the radio. Why? Because you want to pay single-minded attention to the task of finding your way. The second "task" of listening to the radio detracts from the attention you can pay to the task of finding your way.

Or imagine playing tennis. You hit the ball and immediately get ready to make your next shot. You focus single-mindedly on the ball; the better the player you are, the more focused you become. You put all your energy, experience, instinct, and thought into each shot as well as the shot you plan to hit next and what you imagine your opponent will do. The game becomes mental as well as physical, like human chess.

Now imagine playing tennis with two balls. You have to keep track of both, running each down, watching your opponent do the same, as you frantically try to keep two balls in play at once. There is no way your game with two balls could be as good as your game with one.

Multitasking is like playing tennis with two balls, or three, or four. Some people say they pay better attention when they multitask. For a person to do better performing two tasks at once, it must mean that she was not fully engaged with the first task and needed two tasks to get her adrenaline flowing, thus boosting her performance. While this can happen, it would make more sense to try to fully engage with the first task.

That modern life forces a person to perform several tasks seemingly at once may well be true. But it is a myth that you can perform two tasks simultaneously as well as you can perform one. It is fine to believe that multitasking is a skill necessary in the modern world, but to believe it is an equivalent substitute for single-minded focus on one task is incorrect.

It may be convenient or necessary to multitask, to talk on the telephone as you write an e-mail and watch the stock prices stream across your computer screen; or to put clothes in the dryer as you play with your toddler and talk to your real estate agent on the phone. However, you will not be doing any of those tasks as effectively as you would if you were doing them one at a time.

The adrenaline rush you get from the excitement of multitasking may help you in the short run, but it cannot be sustained. Furthermore, even when the adrenaline is at its peak, your performance doing three tasks at once will not be as good as if you were doing just one.

Multitasking can get you into trouble when the tasks are important. I have a lawyer friend who told me how he negotiated an extraordinary deal for himself with several adversaries. He got concessions he never had thought possible. When they reconvened the following year to discuss business, the adversaries asked my friend how on earth he had persuaded them to consent to a deal that was so lopsided against them. He told them he had given the negotiation his full attention, while they had all been pecking away on their BlackBerrys. They had consented to what he proposed without fully focusing on what they were consenting to. It was all legal but done under the influence of BlackBerrys.

Each time you introduce a new object of attention into what you are doing, you dilute your attention on any one object. If, say, you are talking on the telephone and writing an e-mail, neither task receives the benefit of your full attention. As you blip back and forth between the two, you are liable to miss an item in one task while you are blipped over to the other task, just as my friend's adversaries did at their meeting while they worked on their BlackBerrys.

The time you spend on one task may be brief—say, one second or one-tenth of one second—before you switch to another, but at no time are you truly multitasking. You are only doing a series of tasks in rapid sequence, one after the other, over and over again. You may be able to watch four television shows at once, but this is only because you are good at inferring what you missed on one when you come back to it later. You may be able to carry on four conversations simultaneously, but again, you will necessarily miss bits of each. You may pull it off, but no conversation will get your full attention.

If none of what you are doing requires your full attention, it is fine to multitask. Just be aware that you may make mistakes, miss key bits of information, be impolite, and fail to produce your best work.

Sometimes people do what is (erroneously) called multitasking because each of the activities is so boring, they want to do them in rapid succession to bring some excitement to the process, as if playing tennis with one ball were just too dull. Perhaps if your opponent is inferior, it might make sense for you to have to hit two balls and she just one. This is fine, as long as none of what you are doing is important.

But sometimes people try to play tennis with two balls in big matches against strong opponents. They want to be able to switch from one task to another the minute the first task becomes difficult. Instead of bearing with the difficult task, running down the tough shot, or sitting back and thinking about the problem, they simply hop off to a new task and hit the second ball. By the end of the day, they have done a lot of mediocre work and lost the match.

Multitasking ineffectively—what I call "frazzing"—is a common mistake that busy people make, frantically hoping that will work. If the task matters, it is better that you do it by itself. That way you can give it your full attention.

There is an exception. You can ride a bicycle and ponder quantum mechanics at the same time. If you're good, you could ride a bicycle and mix pancake batter at the same time. This is because the riding of the bicycle is done on automatic pilot. You have practiced riding bikes long enough for the skill to be embedded in your brain's automatic pilot, the cerebellum (more on this later).

If you have practiced a piece on the piano long enough, you could play it and read a book at the same time. You lose something, though: It is unlikely the piece would be played as beautifully as if you were giving it your full attention. The shadings and expressions that make a piece of music beautiful require conscious attention, not just automatic pilot. There is an energy, only partly understood, that conscious human attention alone can convey. That's why human interactions convey emotion far more vividly than electronic.

While there is a place for what is commonly called multitasking, the notion that it is as effective as single tasking is wrong. When what you are doing is important, multitasking is a practice to be avoided. Just think of it as playing tennis with two balls.

6 Racing to Get There: The Daily Drill

Julie looked up from her computer screen, glanced at the clock on her desk, and to her horror saw that it was 7:05 p.m. She was supposed to be in Cambridge at 7:15—from downtown Boston, an impossibility. It would probably take that long just to get to her car.

Her brain started to overheat. A familiar toxic feeling, signaling the beginning of the escalating frenzy that had become so frequent in her daily life. Frantically, she stabbed at numbers on her cell phone, then stuffed her briefcase with documents from around her office as if they were pieces of laundry, put the cell phone to her ear, and raced out of her office toward the elevator. "Angela?"

"Yes," came the reply.

"Thank God you're there. You are so reliable. I love you. Are the kids okay?"

"Oh, yes, Mrs. Bennett, they're fine. They're all eating dinner now. They wanted mac and cheese, so I gave it to them. I hope that's all right."

"Anything you do is all right. It's fabulous. I'm late for

dinner with Pete. He will hold it against me for six months if I'm not there soon. Say a prayer for me, Angela."

"Yes, Mrs. Bennett, I will, but don't you worry. Mr. Bennett will understand."

"Thanks, Angela. You're a godsend. We should be home by ten or so."

Just as the elevator doors opened, Julie realized she had left her jacket hanging on the hook of her office door. Her car keys were *in the jacket*. Angrily, she dropped her briefcase at the side of the elevator doors and sprinted down the corridor back into her office. She grabbed her jacket, practically tearing it off the hook, all the while muttering the expletive she always muttered when she was starting to go crazy.

Back to the elevator, down to the car, lurching into reverse, barely missing the massive pillar next to where she parked, then speeding around the spiral down ramp, screeching on the brakes to stop and slide her card into the slot so the barrier would rise, accelerating out onto Cambridge Street, past Massachusetts General Hospital, onto Storrow Drive, which would lead her back to Cambridge. Thank God there's no Red Sox game tonight, she thought.

Safely on Storrow, Julie took a deep breath and, shifting her eyes quickly between the road and her cell phone, punched up Pete's number, praying he would answer. He usually kept his cell phone in the car, refusing to carry it on his person, as he thought it was too much of an intrusion on his time to be always available. No answer. Damn, she thought. He must be at the restaurant already. This is too much. I can't stand it. He is going to give me that look that says, If you really wanted to be here on time, you would have been. I am just not the priority in your life that I used to be.

Julie was coming apart inside. Self-reproach scissored through her mind, slicing her self-esteem until it was in bloody shreds. Gripping the steering wheel so tightly that her knuckles were pearly, she said to herself, Bad wife, bad mother, bad woman, selfish, bad, stupid, ugly, fat . . .

That she weighed 120 pounds and was unarguably attractive made no difference when she was in this state. After turning off Storrow at the Harvard Square exit, she drove over the bridge as fast as the traffic would allow and headed for the Church Street garage. At least I have his present, she thought. A couple of drinks, then I'll hand him the box, and we will be back in love. Unless we're divorced.

As she was leaving her car for the attendant to park, she reached over to the glove compartment to get Pete's present. It wasn't there. Frantically, she looked on the floor, in the backseat, on the dashboard, in her purse, and in her briefcase, crazily dumping the contents of both onto the seat. The present wasn't there. Then she saw it. It was on the kitchen counter at home where she had set it down that morning, saying to herself, Don't forget this, as she'd hurried upstairs to get the tickets she had promised to bring Danny. But once she had picked up the tickets, she had run downstairs and out the door, hurrying into her car so she would be not too late for work — forgetting the box that contained Pete's present.

Julie looked at the parking attendant who had watched this little drama unfold. He was staring at the bizarre pile of stuff on the passenger seat, created by the disgorgement of briefcase and purse. "It's all right," she said to him. "I'm not crazy. Please just take the car. I'll pick up the mess when I come back." She gave him her keys and started to run down Church Street toward the Harvest restaurant, the scene of her first date with Pete, the site of their dinner tonight.

At the door of the restaurant she paused, straightened her

hair, smoothed her jacket and skirt, and glanced at her watch: 7:45. Taking a deep breath and letting it out, she strode into the restaurant, looking for Pete's face, wondering what excuse she would dream up on the spur of the moment. This was so bad, it seemed almost funny.

Unable to locate Pete, she asked the maître d' where Mr. Bennett was sitting. After running his finger down the list of reservations, the maître d' replied, "Madam, he has not yet arrived. May I seat you, or would you like to wait for him here or at the bar?"

"Thank God he's not here," Julie said out loud. The maître d' gave her a puzzled look. "Oh, no, I mean I'm sure he'll be here soon. I'll just take a seat by the bar. Let him know where I am when he arrives."

"Of course," the maître d' said, and turned to greet another couple.

Pete arrived at 8:00 in full fluster, apologies spilling from his lips like a drink gulped too fast. Julie was only too pleased to hear these words and to accept them graciously. "I understand, sweetheart," she said in a lovingly reassuring tone, giving him a kiss on his cheek and a little pat on his butt.

"You wouldn't believe . . . ," Pete began.

"Oh yes, yes, I would," Julie said, putting a finger to Pete's lips. "Our lives are crazy, aren't they?"

"I'm so glad you understand," Pete said. "I thought you'd be angry. I just couldn't get out of the office. One thing led to another. You wouldn't believe—"

"We're in this together," Julie interrupted. "Believe me, I understand." The waiter appeared, and they ordered two drinks, martinis for both.

"You've gotta hear this," Pete began after the drinks had

been ordered. "Banks is totally gone. It's a whole new world. It's like he never even existed. And all that stuff I was trying to digest for the past six months—gonzo. Kaput. Nyet. Nada. Now we have something called GISMO. Stands for gestational information system marketing opportunity. Something about how information goes through like a pregnancy or a period of gestation from conception to delivery and how we can take advantage of that. None of us has any idea what it means. But the guy they brought in who made it up, this guy's a freakin' genius. I'm telling you, Julie, he's crazy-smart. He explained GISMO to us, and of course I didn't get it, but what I could get was how brilliant and totally ahead of its time the idea is. You know how you can sense that kind of thing?" Julie smiled and nodded, basking in the relief she felt of having escaped a disaster. "Well, this idea is gonna rock the marketing world. I know it. And I want to be in the front of the line. So, more work. More change. Are you worried?"

Julie, still smiling, told the truth. "A bit. How about you?"

"A bit," Pete admitted. "Well, a lot. But I'm psyched, Julie. This could be big. And, of course, I have more on my plate than I can handle. Life's just kinda weird these days."

Life these days *is* kinda weird. Lingering is a lost art. Such is our hurry and our need for constant stimulation that a modern romantic conversation might go like this:

"I love you."

"Oh, good. Now, what's your next point?"

Everyone's this busy not (usually) because they want to be or planned to be, but because they can't find a way not to be and still keep up. Being extraordinarily busy—and at times frantic—appears to be the inevitable, uncontrollable consequence of living in today's world. If being busier than I'd like to be is the price I have to pay, most of us seem to say, then so be it. After all, modern life is worth it. Life's never been this exciting.

But if we're not careful, we'll get so busy that we'll miss taking the time to think and to feel. We won't have the extended periods of time required to complete a thought, develop a conversation, or reflect upon a complex set of emotions.

This is already happening. Everyone's attention span is shrinking because our attention has more possible targets than ever before, while more thieves try to steal our attention than we are able to fend off. This leads many people to carry an invisible blipper in their brains, changing stations the minute a conversation, project, thought, or event takes too much time or becomes the least bit boring or taxing. It's not that people are being rude, it's just that there's too much to do and not enough time in which to do it. No one pauses over anything, as if we all have attention deficit disorder.

We're so busy that we risk not taking advantage of the many unexpected opportunities that beckon. When it comes to our new technology, we're like kids who just got their driver's licenses, wanting to drive constantly, even when we don't have a destination in mind, just loving the newfound freedom of the open road.

Watch people on their cell phones or BlackBerrys as they walk down Fifth Avenue or wait in airport lounges; there's still a little bit of a kid at play in there. Talk on the phone as you walk down the street? Awesome, dude! Way cool. I can't believe I can really do this! Look at those people walking by me looking at me as I talk on my phone. I bet they all wish they had one as cool as mine.

Watch the stock trader multitasking, shifting from his phone to his e-mail to the streaming stock quotes on his Bloomberg to typing on his PC to talking to someone who pops his head in the door. This orchestration of activities is nothing if not thrilling, at least for most of the people who do it (and call it work). Watch a sixteen-year-old girl instant messaging—of course, I should say, IM'ing—as fast as most people can talk; this girl has found heaven. Watch a forty-five-year-old man playing on his son's Game Boy, practicing, trying to get good enough to beat his son; that won't happen, but Dad is having a ball trying. Watch the journalist putting together an article, finding in milliseconds on a Google search what used to take hours or days to research, cutting and pasting in seconds what used to take many minutes and painstaking attention to accomplish. Watch the modern mom coordinating the schedules of five children, one husband, two pets, and herself; how did she ever do it before cell phones, e-mail, and voice mail? As harried as she is, she is not bored. A part of her feels like a master of her universe, making good on a difficult task.

Now that we have our licenses and our cars, we want to drive. There're so many of us new drivers that it's a bit like bumper cars out there, bumping into one another as we talk on our cells, backing up into one another as we check e-mail on our BlackBerrys. Pushing the limits of how much we can do is exhilarating. It can also be exhausting, misguided, and potentially dangerous (for instance, cell phones while driving), but there's no turning back now. Nor do we want to. It's such fun. Yeah, and kinda weird.

7 Energy, Enthusiasm, and Play

Today's energy explodes everywhere. It is the energy of the newsroom at deadline, the courtroom during intense cross examination, the emergency room when three crisis cases arrive at once, the fire station when an alarm comes in, or the racetrack as the horses round the turn and down the stretch they come.

Today's enthusiasm packs the power to break traditions and tear down barriers. It is not just technology that has flattened the world, to use Thomas Friedman's metaphor, it is the renegade spirit it let loose. This is not the renegade spirit of the radicals from the 1960s; far from it. It is the renegade spirit of people who love to play—with ideas, with numbers, with algorithms, with programs. At the very core of what they did and do is play, letting their imaginations take them where it will and let the way it's always been done be damned. Embracing change, not fearing it, today's enthusiasm sets minds free.

In another of the many paradoxes of this peculiar age, it is the nerds and wonks at play who turned out to be the most effective radicals, if you define radical as a person who changes things fundamentally. The suits and ties snapped up what the nerds and wonks in sweats and sneakers brought forth, but none of this would have happened were it not for the nerds and wonks. If hip means ahead of the crowd, the nerds and wonks are the hippest of all.

When social critics deplore the materialism of our time and its preoccupation with money, fame, and superficial values, they overlook that the driving force behind the changes we have seen—one of the greatest periods of change in history—has been thought. It wasn't big bucks or social status that drove this change. It was, and is, the force of the play of the mind. As materialistic as we may be, playful thinking got us here.

Baffling as it can be, this world is a new mother lode, packing more opportunities than we can possibly mine as old, formerly impassable barriers to the mine fall apart. We now can mine a volume of accessible information that gives to every individual mind the power of what it used to take hundreds of minds to do. We can work with an ease and speed of communication that makes the dead time called "waiting" obsolete, or at least unnecessary. These elements create the peculiar enthusiasm of our time. Like cave people finding fire, we're amazed and excited to use our new tools. A new kind of fire blazes in this world.

Those who cling to old ways get burned. Those who crave security and fear change lobby for a pension that, as it turns out, they can't depend upon. If you want to take advantage of what today's world has to offer, you have to live by your wits and be willing to try something new, leaving your comfort zone for a while.

The enthusiasm that characterizes our time is, unlike current events, hopeful and, like all enthusiasms, playful. The energy that flashes through our electronics has leapt into most of our bloodstreams and brains. For all the difficulties we contend with, we wouldn't turn back the clock from digital to analog for all the tea in China. Indeed, China is such a part of this new world that its tea is the least of what we want from over there. We want to hold on to this new world that China, India, America, and the rest of the wired world is fast creating, without even knowing what it is creating.

When you get close to the excitement, it can feel crazed, yet at its best it is white hot with concentrated, focused energy— creative, synthetic, innovative, impatient, irreverent, and breath-taking. The feeling this life can induce if you go with it is like the gut-in-your-mouth feeling you get when you are in free fall while, say, skiing, or in a skid on the highway, or in the midst of a deal that is taking you faster than you can consciously reckon with but hope it's taking you where you want to go.

You are totally focused. You don't know what you're doing, as you have lost all self-consciousness. In this frame of mind, we are in what Mihaly Csikszentmihalyi has shown to be our state of highest functioning as well as greatest joy, a state he named "flow" and about which he wrote a book by the same name. In flow, we rely on the special talent Malcolm Gladwell described in his book *Blink: The Ability to Think Without Thinking*.

Both flow and blink catch chunks of what is unique in modern life. Although throughout history both the state of flow and the talent of blink have been with us, never before have they been so prominent and useful in daily life.

Formerly locked in place, the modern individual has been tossed up into the air. Today, victory belongs to those who don't freeze up when cast aloft but instead figure out how to fly, or at least how to get back up after they fall.

Old habits and strategies don't apply. In addition to the books about flow and blink, other influential books about modern culture point up what a counterintuitive, radically new era we live in. Even the titles of some of the best books suggest the paradoxical, seemingly insane nature of modern life: *The World Is Flat*; *Everything Bad Is Good for You*; *Freakonomics*; *The Progress Paradox*; *Out of Our Minds*; *Perfect Madness*; and *A Whole New Mind*.

No one knows quite what to expect anymore, and what they do expect won't happen quite as expected. What's good for you today will be discovered to be bad tomorrow and vice versa. Information travels so fast, it outstrips disagreement and research. Yesterday we were told to take vitamin E; today, don't; tomorrow, perhaps do. Don't drink coffee, we were told; now, do, but just the right amount, which is called "moderate."

Even what everyone agrees is good for you can seem to contradict itself. For example, how do you both get enough sleep and make every minute count? Or how do you follow your bliss but be practical in preparing for the world that lies ahead? And how do you floss regularly, eat eight servings of fruits and vegetables a day, drink lots of water, exercise at least thirty minutes at least three times a week, attend religious services regularly, belong to groups that matter to you and attend their meetings, keep up with your friends, not neglect your outside interests, work your job, raise your kids, do the laundry, pay taxes, have sex at least once a week, deal with the pressure of relentless uncertainty, and change the oil in your car every three thousand miles without possessing the powers of a miracle maker? No one knows. From corporate strategies to child-rearing theories to personal health to money management to career expectations, uncertainty rules.

But also, opportunity knocks. The old is out, and the new has yet to stabilize or define itself. Life is wide open.

8 Oxymorons of Modern Life: Connected Anonymity and Social Disconnection

On the one hand, life today can be as exhilarating as a dangerous game, an X-Game. We are pumped. Adrenaline is the hormone of our times, and caffeine is our favorite drug. Opportunities open as fast as doors close. Busy has banished boredom. From Match.com to Google to eBay to Craigslist to saveadog.com, you can find a romantic partner, find a business opportunity, find a pet, get tickets to the Red Sox, or buy a car, all in the space of minutes, without leaving your desk. You can e-mail your daughter who's studying in India or be instantly in touch with your eccentric friend who won't tell you where he lives but will give you his e-mail address.

The behavior of that eccentric friend defines another prevalent paradox: connected anonymity. A person can connect online intimately while remaining completely anonymous. People used to be able to do this only at masked balls. Then, decades ago, automobiles introduced us to a version of connected anonymity on a wide scale; people could drive without being recognized while connecting recklessly or rudely with other drivers. But that was nothing compared with what is possible today. The electronic age has taken connected anonymity to a whole new level, for better and worse.

While connected anonymity may be ominous at times, it can also be useful, as when a person participates in a blog. However, a deadly paradox does permeate our busy world. While we have been miraculously connecting electronically over the past fifteen years, we have also quietly and unintentionally been disconnecting interpersonally. Neighborhoods, clubs, organizations, and even friendships do not hold our attention as they once did. Family dinner has become a nice idea that's hard to make happen. Lunch with a friend, conversation over the back fence, or sitting on the stoop saying hi to the passersby has given way to busier, individual pursuits. As Robert Putnam pointed out in his 2000 book, *Bowling Alone*, more people are bowling than ever, but participation in teams has declined. People are bowling alone.

Such social disconnection exacts an unrecognized price, leading to most of the varieties of unhappiness we see today but blame on other causes. Virtually every person who consults me as a psychiatrist suffers from some form of disconnection, although he or she does not label it as such. Interpersonal disconnection and social isolation lead to or exacerbate depression, drug and alcohol abuse, anxiety, poor tolerance of frustration, and a tendency toward violent behavior. Furthermore, the feeling of being more alone than you'd like to be — disconnection — hinders performance at work or school and reduces the sense of well-being and joy in life. Finally, it attacks your body, reducing immune function and actually lowering life expectancy. When Dr. Lisa Berkman first proved this in her landmark study from the 1970s, few people believed that death could be caused by disconnectedness or social isolation. Now, having been proven in a dozen other studies both in the United States and abroad, it is an accepted fact that social isolation ranks up there with cigarette smoking, high cholesterol, and high blood pressure as risk factors for an early demise.

When people comment on the perils and possibilities of modern life, they usually skip over these crucial ones: the damages done by disconnecting as well as the benefits conferred by connecting.

Now we often settle for the illusion of the human connection. People tune in to the *Today* show and greet the hosts as if they knew them personally. They smile back at Katie Couric's smile as if Katie were a close friend; they look forward to seeing Matt, calling him "Matt" as if he also knew their name; they wait for Al to say, "And here's what's happening in your neck of the woods," as if he actually cared about the weather in their neck of the woods. They get the warm feeling that comes from connection the same way trompe l'oeil imparts the feeling of three dimensions. Close inspection, however, reveals that it's a trick.

A lady's computerized voice speaks to you on the telephone, offering you in the most accommodating, polite, albeit inhuman tone a decision tree into which you can climb to try to find what you need. If you do get a human being, it is likely a stranger in India—made to sound as if he is just down the street—who has been instructed to tell you that his name is Joe or Tom to create the illusion that he is like you. Actual human beings greet you at the ticket counter at the movie theater, but they have been instructed to become inhuman by parroting an embarrassing preamble like "Welcome to Loew's, and may I tell you about our Super Saver that includes a jumbo drink and a jumbo popcorn, both refillable, or a bottled water if you prefer?" While you ask for two tickets to *Star Wars*, you get the strange feeling of indigestion and alienation that is so common in modern life, derived from interacting with a person who has been forced to behave like a recording. It is akin to how you feel when politicians tell you what you desperately want to hear, but you know it has been rehearsed. These are people trying (and failing) to create the illusion of genuine connection. It is not the illusion that we need. We need the real thing.

9 Scheduled Lovemaking

The real thing—genuine, human connection—is still available, but it's best to book it into your schedule. What isn't booked often doesn't happen. You may intend to keep up with a friend, but if you don't schedule a time to see him or her, you may unwittingly put it off for years. You may intend to "do lunch" with your old roommate, but this won't happen if you just wait for it to. "Unnecessary" social engagements often end up where the cartoon caption put them: "Lunch Thursday? Thursday's no good for me. How about never? How's never for you?"

Waiting for things to happen on their own might have worked in the past, but no longer. It may sound strange, but I have even advised some of my busiest patients to schedule lovemaking. At first they protest, How unromantic! But then I remind them that by using their current "romantic" schedule, they hardly ever make love anymore. They complain they'd like to make love more often and don't understand why it doesn't happen. Before they blame each other, I suggest they make a date to make love. While this may sound unromantic, it isn't. If today is Tuesday and you have a date with your mate to make love on Thursday evening at nine, the erotic anticipation can begin right now. Far from being unromantic, it is highly romantic and quite a turn-on for most people.

In the rush of today's world, you need a plan to make sure you stay genuinely connected with living humans you know and like. Easy? Just count the number of minutes you spend each day with live human beings, in person, people you know and like. Compare that number with, say, twenty years ago or even ten. If you're like most people, today's number is dramatically lower. That's not good for our mental or physical health. Disconnectedness is a lethal danger lurking behind the obvious dangers in this busy world.

Of course, some of our discomfort derives simply from not understanding what's going on. I watch my daughter manipulating her thumbs around the keys of her cell phone faster than I can type, and when I ask her what she is doing, she looks at me as if I'm from Mars, and I learn for the first time about instant messaging, or IM. I begin to shake my head in the same baffled way my parents did when they first saw and heard the Beatles. This all takes some getting used to.

But we also have to be able to stick up for ourselves and not blandly accept whatever is thrust at us. The rush and the gush of modern life can also steamroll your feelings, pressuring you to accept disconnectedness without protest. A doctor speaks to you for fifteen seconds before sending you elsewhere for "a test" that he will review "later" before he gets back to you. When you see him next, he announces that you have cancer, explains to you what kind of cancer it is, how he knows you have it, what the survival statistics are on it, and what treatment he recommends, all in the space of *ten minutes*, after which he refers you to another doctor, an oncologist, who may or may not take some time to get to know you just a little bit while you entrust him with the hope that he will save your life. Worry. Gush. Rush. All smeared with blather.

This life begets confusion. After you express your concern many times that your fifth-grade son is underachieving and may have a learning disability, your son works his way up the ranks of the many others in line and is given "a formal evaluation." The school psychologist then calls you in for a meeting with a panel of "experts," all of whom stare at you blankly from across a table while you hear the results of "the testing." You find it "did not reveal any condition warranting special help or accommodations." You are then presented with a written report running some fifteen pages that are full of numbers and data that you can't comprehend and you are curtly told you have "the right to appeal." When you state that you didn't think of this as a legal proceeding, you are told "the committee" has many other cases to attend to and that this meeting is over. Worry. Gush. Rush. And lots of blather.

10 Emotion: Key #1 to the Best of Modern Life

The forgotten key to taking advantage of the best in modern life is not intellectual but emotional. It is not that the intellect doesn't matter. It has never mattered more. But emotion is the on/off switch for advanced thinking. Oddly, that's what so many people ignore, from managers in the workplace, to teachers in the classroom, to husbands and wives trying to get done what needs to get done to make a household run. They jump right into the morass of tasks that must be attended to, without first creating the emotional conditions under which the doing of those tasks will flow fluidly and flourish.

Hope, optimism, confidence, and enthusiasm—positive emotional energy—make for happiness and success these days, just as they always have done. The difference now is that it is especially difficult to maintain those attitudes because everyone is in such a hurry.

How much better do you feel at the start of a meeting if you get a strong handshake and honest eye contact? How much more enthusiastic do you feel if your host puts you at ease by making a few personal remarks or noticing how healthy you look? These niceties matter far more than merely being "nice." They can make or break a deal, a relationship, or a project. They set a positive emotional tone, which in turn brings out the best in people.

Most current advice related to the problems of modern life focuses on the need to get organized. Indeed, as one person said to me, getting organized has become the modern form of dieting: Everyone wants to do it, few do it successfully, and even those who do do it successfully usually revert to their former state. While disorganization is an important problem, it is not the root of the matter, any more than losing weight is the key to happiness. Just as you can be thin and miserable, you can be very well organized and still feel overwhelmed by modern life.

At the heart of making the most of life today is the ability to treasure and protect your connections to what you care most about: people, places, activities, pets, a spiritual connection, a piece of music, even objects that are dear to you. But you must not have too many connections or none will flourish. Pick the ones that matter most to you and nourish them religiously; make that your top priority in life, and you can't go wrong.

Today, the rush and the gush threaten to attenuate or even destroy our most important connections. Unless you consciously and deliberately preserve time for, say, family dinner, or lunch with a friend, or Sunday dinner at Grandma's, or a weekend away with your spouse, or physical exercise, or playing the instrument you love, or keeping up with the team you have always followed, or taking your dog for a walk, or going to your son's or daughter's play or game, or weeding the garden you so adore, or working on your boat, or reading journals about underwater welding—unless you consciously and deliberately preserve time to connect with what matters most to *you*, your connection with whatever it is will erode. The waters of the rush and the gush will rust it out and sweep it away. You will find yourself less energetic, less optimistic, less hopeful, less confident, and less enthusiastic than before, and you won't know why. You'll ascribe it to being too busy or to growing older, or depression, or being too disorganized, or just to "life."

The true culprit is neither disorganization nor any of the other possible culprits just mentioned. It is that you have neglected what matters most to you. In this era, you *must* deliberately preserve and cultivate your most valuable connections to people, activities, and whatever else is most important to you. Anyone can cultivate these connections, drawing from them the strength and will a person needs to handle the best and worst of life, *but only if you plan to do so and insist on adhering to your plan.*

The next step in promoting and preserving important connections is selection. Connections are like flowers in a garden. If you overplant, none will thrive. If you let weeds grow, the flowers will fade. Two of the most difficult tasks you do are holding the line on how many connections you commit to and weeding out the bad connections. But only by selecting with care to what and to whom you want to give your precious time, attention, and energy will you be able to maintain a positive emotional state and do your best.

This principle applies to your professional life as well as your personal. Studies of successful people in business—as, for example, in the book *Good to Great* or from Jack Welch's account of his days at General Electric—emphasize the importance of focusing on what you do best and sticking with it. Don't try to do too much, or you will do nothing well. In today's great buffet of opportunities, it is easy for the eyes to grow bigger than the stomach.

The same principle of selection makes or breaks personal

fulfillment. You simply can't keep up with too large a number of friends. If there are too many, they all become burdens rather than joys as you labor to stay in touch with the multitude. Selection may seem cruel at first, but in the long run it is not only essential but kind, both to you and to the other person.

To summarize, positive emotion matters more than people realize. Usually regarded as a result rather than a cause, positive emotion is in fact a powerful cause of good results of any kind. And the key to positive emotion is not merely getting organized — although that can help — but also maintaining your connections to what matters most to you. This in turn requires that you select the connections you care most about and cultivate just those. In so doing, you will create the positive emotional state that will allow you best to deploy your time, attention, and energy.

11 Rhythm: Key #2 to the Best of Modern Life

Some people date the start of modern life with the advent of air-conditioning, because air-conditioning allowed people to go indoors instead of sitting out on the stoop talking with one another. Going indoors marked the beginning of connected anonymity and social disconnection. As for me, I discovered modern life on weeknights between 3:00 a.m. and 6:00 a.m. in 1970 when I was twenty years old, working a summer job as a short-order cook at a now defunct greasy spoon just off Route 2, near Boston. Part roadside diner and part doughnut bakery, it was a favorite of truck drivers in the wee hours. I worked the wee hours, midnight to 8:00 a.m., but it was from 3:00 a.m. to 6:00 a.m. that I discovered modern life, because during those hours I had no help.

When the place filled up, I could have a dozen orders at a time on the grill. Burgers, hot dogs, grilled cheese sandwiches, eggs, bacon, sausages, hash browns, pancakes, French toast, western omelets, and the occasional cube steak would be deployed around my grill as I quickly shifted focus from egg to pancake to burger to batter bowl to butter brush, directing my attention according to the look and sound of each item as it cooked, as well as my sense of how long it had been cooking.

I could never totally focus on tending the grill because between 3:00 a.m. and 6:00 a.m., there were no waitresses or waiters to take new orders and respond to requests from the customers. I was the only one there for those three hours, aside from the baker in back, whose sole and simple duty it was to make the doughnuts, and Doris at the register, whose sole and even simpler job it was to guard the cash and make change. How often I wished they would come help me, but that was not their job, and they would have gotten in trouble had they done so. The owner was adamant. The baker was there to make the doughnuts, Doris was there to guard the cash, and between 3:00 a.m. and 6:00 a.m., I did the rest. Around 6:00 a.m. reinforcements arrived, so I could finally slow down.

Between 3:00 and 6:00, I learned how to pay attention to more than I ever had simultaneously paid attention to before. As I stood at the grill, one part of my mind had to sense what was going on behind me while the rest of me kept track of the grill and stole glances at the dupes hanging down from the clips above me. Each time I'd take a new order, I'd write it down on a pad that had a piece of carbon paper that I'd place between the first sheet and the second. The first sheet was the customer's copy, which he'd take to Doris. The second was the dupe, or duplicate, which I'd hang above the grill to remind me what to cook and for whom. I had to be looking down—on the grill— up—at the dupes—and sensing what was behind—at the counter with the customers. Down, up, and behind. It became a kind of rhythm that once I got into would carry me along like a song.

When business was slow, which was most of the time between 3:00 a.m. and 5:00 a.m., with only a few potheads seeking munchies coming in or the odd loner, partygoer, or trucker looking for a pit stop, it was easy to take orders and tend the grill. But starting around 5:00 a.m., and on some days earlier than that, the trucks and early commuters would stream in. Business picked up in a hurry.

Having to go faster and faster, I would try to use my rhythm like an automatic pilot, so I could save conscious attention to focus on what was not automatic—taking a new order, placing the right food on the right plate, and delivering plates to the right stool. Using automatic pilot, I could let the cracking of the eggs, the ladling of the pancake batter, the swiping the toast with the butter brush, and the turning of the mound of hash browns get done without my having to plan. It was a difficult job. Like an athlete grown old, I couldn't do it today.

Rhythm was key. When I kept my rhythm, I could do the job effortlessly. But whenever I got out of synch and let myself get overloaded, I'd crash. My automatic pilot ceased functioning, and I would lose track of whose order was whose and which pancakes I'd put on the grill first. I'd keep one customer waiting forever while attending to another customer out of turn, then take up more time apologizing to the waiting customer while eggs would overcook, pancakes would burn, and uncooked hash browns would sit cold, waiting for me to put them on the grill. Once I lost my rhythm, it could take half an hour to get it back. I'd have angry customers and no tips.

I learned that I had a maximum. As the summer went on and I gained skill, my maximum increased, but there was always a maximum beyond which I could not work well. I learned to sense when I reached it. As long as I could still "see" the counter out of the eyes in the back of my head while I was at the grill, I was all right. But when I lost that sense of what was going on behind me, I knew I had to slow down right away and take stock, or in a matter of seconds I would be out of synch and in serious trouble.

If I didn't slow down at that point, I'd get worked up. Anxiety would splinter my concentration, breaking my rhythm. My confidence would plummet, and I would quickly start making mistakes, which, of course, would lead me to make more mistakes.

If I let the job control me, if I let the customers set the pace, if I responded to every request immediately and tried to put out every order as if it were the only order on the grill and there was but one customer to wait on, I was doomed. But if I took control, if I let my instincts as well as my knowledge and experience guide me, if I followed a plan but also didn't overthink it, and instead trusted myself even when I wasn't consciously dictating all of what I was doing, then I could get the job done well.

Over the course of the summer, I learned how to orchestrate the job's many demands. I learned how to prioritize on the go, instinctively, and defer what could be deferred by, say, pushing the hash browns to the side or giving a new customer a newspaper as I told him he'd have to wait five minutes. I learned how to integrate my conscious brain with my automatic brain, and I learned how to spot the moment when I had reached my limit, a moment at which I had to slow down.

I also discovered what a kick it is to rule over such chaos, to do a complex task well, faster and faster.

What I didn't realize was that I was learning about what life would be like in the 2000s. Standing at that grill, keeping track of random demands coming from behind me, being responsible for time-sensitive tasks and items that could burn up if I didn't watch out, getting into a rhythm of managing it, and feeling elated when it all harmonized — that resembles what most adults who work now do every day, as well as most parents and children.

"Rhythm" is my word for the complex set of neurological and physiological events that create the *apparent* effortlessness of a person doing complicated work well: me at the grill or you doing whatever you do best. You probably make it *look* easy. But it took you years of practice to get there. If you have ever watched a professional golfer on TV, you have probably remarked on how easy he or she makes it look. If you have watched a pianist, you may have wondered how he or she coordinates those finger movements so fluidly.

As a person practices any activity, the planning and executing of it moves gradually from one part of the brain to another. At the beginning, it is all in the frontal lobes. Each movement has to be monitored consciously and deliberately. But with practice — often arduous practice — the activity gets rooted in the back of the brain at the cerebellum. The cerebellum is the automatic pilot of the brain.

The example everyone knows about is riding a bike. At the beginning you are shaky, monitoring each movement and falling off. But over time, riding the bike becomes automatic. The cerebellum has taken over. Now you can use your frontal lobes to watch the sights or plan where you want to ride to.

But what about busy modern life? That's not one task, like a golf swing, a certain piano piece, or riding a bike. It's many, disparate tasks. That's why the cerebellum can't run the whole show. Nor would you want it to. You wouldn't want to live your life on automatic pilot. Conscious, deliberate choice is essential.

When you are in what I call a rhythm, you are somewhere in between cerebellar-mediated automatic pilot and total frontal lobe control. Some of what you are doing—buttering the toast, cracking the eggs—is done automatically. But some of it you deliberately decide to do—which customer to wait on next, what to say to the man who complains that his coffee is too weak.

In coming sections, I will offer many suggestions about the deliberate and conscious part of making the most of busy, modern life. I will emphasize the need for a deliberately formulated plan. I will give the topic of time management minutely detailed attention. I will also give the topic of attention that kind of attention.

But the goal of all the prioritizing and planning is to program you and your brain so that habit, routine, and other automatic functions can take over a big chunk of the work, freeing up your frontal lobes to do the creative, sophisticated work they are uniquely qualified to do. When you find your rhythm, you don't plan everything you're doing; you're just doing it. You'll be in the zone. Just as a pianist who knows a piece so well that his cerebellum takes care of hitting the right notes can devote his conscious attention to other matters like expression and shading, so you can devote your conscious mind to higher issues than the nuts and bolts of each day if you have found the right rhythm for you.

Many elements combine to lead you into the right rhythm, elements that busy life can batter and destroy if you let it. Positive emotional environment. Prioritizing. Planning how you use your time. Getting rid of people and projects that drain you, while cultivating those that are replenishing. Doing what you do best. Practicing. Having time to practice. These elements and others that I will discuss in part 2 combine to lead you into the right rhythm. Then, and only then, can you *effectively* practice the Nike solution: Just do it.

"Just do it" sounds so simple, but it is hugely complex. I am trying to break it down sufficiently so that you can apply it to the busy life you lead. When it works right, "just do it" is the best way to do anything—from playing golf to writing a novel. It never means you don't put effort into what you're doing; it simply means you aren't letting extraneous or fretful thoughts get in your way.

If the frontal lobes are asked to attend to too many details of "just doing it"—buttering the toast, cracking the eggs, balancing the bike, finding F-sharp—they will have no room left for the creative work. That means you will perform at a mediocre level. It also means you will be stressed out, as the frontal lobes don't like monitoring boring, repetitive tasks.

Similarly, the reason I stressed the importance of creating a positive emotional atmosphere wherever you are is that negative emotions also shut down the frontal lobes, making them primitive, costing them the sophistication and creativity they otherwise possess.

You may already have programmed yourself well enough so that you quickly find your rhythm on many days. These are the days when things go well, when you can get everything done with apparent ease and still have time to take a long bath or read a book. These are the days when you swerve and avoid the deer rather than ramming into it; when you field sixteen complaints and make each customer leave happy without losing your cool or steaming inside; when you catch the glass you dropped before it hits the floor; when you don't push the button you shouldn't push and you do push the one you should.

It is impossible to make all this happen consciously. You must rely on your rhythm. You can't stay on top of all the details of life and also be ready for all the opportunities and dangers.

You *have* to rely on rhythm—or some equivalent. Whatever our brains can do and computers can't do, that is what comes to the rescue for us if we allow it to and set up the conditions that favor its growth. I call it rhythm. It is a special force that allows us to do much more than we think. Whatever you call it, you have to develop a force you trust, a force that will guide you to remember what you need to remember, do what you need to do, choose what you need to choose, and avoid what you need to avoid.

Using the suggestions in the later sections of this book, you can sculpt your brain and your day even further, so that more and more can become automatic and operate under positive emotional influences, thus freeing up your creative, sophisticated brain not only to do its best work, but to enjoy it in the process.

Since the human brain has never been as taxed as it is today, this kind of special handling has never been so important.

12 Finding Hope When You're Down

To return to emotion, one of the common problems we face is getting out of bad places. Losing hope is easy these days, because there are so many dangers, so many chances to get lost, make mistakes, or be cut off.

Realistically, there is hope. But emotions often don't recognize reality. As much as the man whose job gets outsourced or offshored may feel out of luck and give up hope, he has more of a chance to rebound than he would have had a generation ago or before that. But he has to feel hopeful to do so. Emotion precedes action. Emotion turns action on or turns it off.

There's a nasty catch-22 embedded here. In order to rebound you need to feel hopeful, but in order to feel hopeful you need to rebound. Where does fresh hope come from when you're fresh out of hope?

From connection. The person who is down will only fall down deeper if he disconnects. On the other hand, if he turns to the connections that matter most to him—a friend, a family member, God, a piece of music, an old mentor, a playing field that's full of good memories, a garden, whatever truly matters—

hope will spark as surely as if flint hit stone. It is the connection that makes the spark. Neither the flint nor the stone does it on its own.

Once the connection is made, positive energy flows instantly. The doorway to advanced thinking opens in the brain. Ideas can now find their way into consciousness.

Today's world favors people who have ideas. If, say, a friend of the man whose job has been outsourced or he himself came up with an idea for a new business, he could take the steps to make it happen more quickly than ever—as long as he believed he could. He could research the idea more quickly, find the money for it more quickly, start it up and see it succeed or fail more quickly, and start another after that more quickly than ever before. The rush and the gush become allies if worry gives way to hope. The forgotten variable—emotion, turning negative emotional energy into positive—is the most crucial of all.

Hucksters have always preached that to succeed all you have to do is want to, but it has rarely been as true as it is today, be it in America, China, or India. If you turn uncertainty and insecurity upside down, opportunities drop out—and this is certainly an uncertain and insecure age. Just as you can never rest easy when you're up these days, you never need to despair when you're down. There's hope—as long as you can keep your hopes up. While hope itself is not a strategy, without it you'll never formulate a good one.

But how difficult it is to feel up when you're down, and how easy it is to feel overwhelmed by the volume, speed, blather, and worry in life, especially when you're down. When you're up, you ride this fast life like a surfer atop a great wave, but when you're down you wipe out.

Our task now is to learn how to use the technology we've invented, rather than allow it to use us, so that it improves our human connections, and does not replace them.

Once the thrill of driving wears off, the teenager gets tired of going just anywhere and becomes more fussy in her choice of destinations. If there's no place special to go, she might just stay at home. We need to learn to be more fussy in how much we log on, watch, transmit, chat, surf, or IM. We need to be careful that we don't allow our electronic devices—and the curious magnetism they exert upon our minds—to take control of us, spurring us to go faster and faster, to do more and more, to track more and more data points, and, in general, to believe that being busy is the enlightened way of life.

Instead, being deeply connected to what matters most is the enlightened way of life.

13 Gemmelsmerch

Busyness can be rhythmic and organized or staccato and random. How you handle the force of distraction becomes crucial in today's world.

Jumping up from the table, talking on the cell phone nonstop, checking messages every hour if not more, rushing off to the next vital appointment—isn't this what important people do? Doesn't being busy mean that you are successful? Actually, not necessarily. Warren Buffett sits at his computerless desk in Nebraska and thinks. Bill Gates takes two weeks off every year to go to a cabin in the woods to . . . think. An unknown but talented poet sits somewhere right now in silence, grappling with his imagination to find the right word. Two lovers sit silently side by side in chairs by a lake right now, connecting intimately without speaking. A ten-year-old boy hovers over a frog he has stalked for the past twenty minutes. Now, he just watches. Rather than capture the frog, he watches. He likes watching it. In fact, busy is not always best.

A force that I call "gemmelsmerch" tugs at our attention all the time. Gemmelsmerch is a meaningless word I made up to describe the ubiquitous force that distracts us from whatever we're doing. Gemmelsmerch works through many channels. Indeed, the many channels on today's television create gemmelsmerch, as we become distracted by the opportunity to watch something else even if we are enjoying what we are watching. What if something better is on? In ages past, we might have wondered if something better was on, but we wouldn't have had three hundred channels to check out the possibility. A better job, a better book, a better restaurant, a better romantic partner—they are all there for our perusal much more immediately than ever before. What a boon! But with this boon comes multifarious gemmelsmerch.

Having treated ADD since 1981, I began to see an upsurge in the mid-1990s in the number of people who complained of being chronically inattentive, disorganized, and overbooked. Many came to me wondering if they had ADD. While some did, most did not. Instead, they had what I called a severe case of modern life. This imitator was not the true, genetically transmitted syndrome of attention deficit disorder, but an environmentally induced stand-in. Because I saw it so often, not only in my practice but in the lives of everyone around me, I started to give this condition names. First I just called it modern life, then pseudo-ADD, then attention deficit trait, and for this book I named it "F-state," because so many of the adjectives one could use to describe it begin with the letter f: frantic, frenzied, forgetful, flummoxed, frustrated, and fragmented, to name a few.

Julie, in the earlier vignette, was catapulted into F-state when she saw she had lost track of the time and was going to be late for her anniversary dinner—only to find that F-state had made her husband late, too. An awful lot of anniversary dinners are not coming off as planned these days. While neither Julie nor the whole nation has ADD, most of us do try to do too much in too little time, which leads to all the f's that make us look like an ADD nation.

In this country especially, modern life offers a feast that, ironically, many people can't find the time to eat. Instead, we run ragged trying to make sure we preserve our places at the table, trying to fulfill all our commitments, afraid that we'll be left out of the banquet if we don't. Owing to the conditioning we've received in the past ten years, some of us are simply *unable* to slow down.

Others frankly don't want to. For them, F-state is *fun*. No one *needs* to read three newspapers every day, check e-mail every ten minutes, make or take scores of phone calls every day, and channel surf during all conversations, tuning out the moment stimulation subsides. These are habits some people develop simply because such habits make them feel charged up, as if doing a lot fast puts them on the cutting edge of life.

In today's world, free time or down time—time to do nothing but just hang out and think or feel or listen and watch—has become as rare as silence. Instead, we hop to. Gotta have action. Keep driving, don't stop for long, don't pause to linger, wonder, or think. Those activities are slow, which is often simply a code word for difficult or demanding. No, the modern imperative is to keep moving, eyes roaming, attention on scan, cell phone in hand.

Look at our popular movies. Long on action, special effects, quick cuts, and fast pace. Short on character. Thought is permissible, but only about twists in plot, not in complications or depth of character. Conversation is okay, but it is best kept to short sentences or phrases, laced with humor, wit, and punch.

In his provocative book *Everything Bad Is Good for You,*

Steven Johnson documents the fact that current television and movies are actually far more cognitively demanding than they were a generation ago, owing to their much faster pace, more intricate plots, and greater number of characters. Many people, myself included, have become so accustomed to action, fast pace, and brisk dialogue in movies that they often avoid movies that are "good" or "deep" because they also fear such movies will bore them, not satisfying their need for speed.

What makes current TV dramas like *Law & Order, CSI,* or *24* cognitively demanding—what leads Steven Johnson to deem them good for us—is not what makes, say, *Hamlet, To Kill a Mockingbird,* or *The Great Gatsby* cognitively demanding. It is not the complexity of character, the ambiguity of theme, the ambivalence of motivation. It is simply the rush and the gush. What holds us is the speed at which data enter the plot, the number of data points we have to then keep track of, and the lack of connectors to make the task easier. We have to work to understand, but not in ways that deepen our lives. These shows are merely difficult to follow. By being difficult to follow, they succeed in their purpose of holding our attention and providing diversion.

You should make sure that you do not do to your life what has been done to modern TV dramas. You should make sure that you do not merely make your life faster and more full of data—more difficult to follow and keep track of—in an effort to make it more fulfilling. While doing so may frantically engage you, much like rushing to catch a plane, it will not deepen you or fulfill you. Quite the opposite.

It would be as if I tried to make this book gripping by electronically causing the words to stream quickly before your eyes or by turning every fourth word into an anagram. Reflexively you would strain to keep up or you would try to sort out each anagram, and you would consider this book very difficult. But that would not make it deep, nor would it give you lasting satisfaction. It would simply appeal to what you have been conditioned to expect: speed and stimulation, the pleasures of sudden wonder.

The rush and the gush have conditioned us all to require more and more speed and stimulation to feel engaged and not bored. Like many people, I take on a lot in my life, too much at times. Reveling in my many tasks and opportunities, loving the rush, I also often have to fight with my schedule to preserve time I value, like time with my family, time with a friend, or time to work out. At times I feel helpless to control the problem of overload that I myself have created—in fact craved.

But I try to remember what the rotary phone taught me. And I try to remember that I do have more control than I often exert.

14 The Paradox of Labor-Saving Devices

From all this busyness, another of the many paradoxes of modern life emerges: The faster we go, the more we take on; and the more we take on, the more there is for us to do. Labor-saving devices thus create more labor. By shortening the time and energy it takes to do any one thing, these devices free up time and energy to do more things.

People have lived fast and taken on a lot in other eras. What is unique to our era is the open access to so much that so many have, all interlinked and growing, second by second. Like a tsunami gathering force, a wall of data gathers above us, ready to crash down and flood our lives, drowning everyone except those who sought the higher ground of uninterrupted, protected time. There the waters can irrigate rather than destroy.

In the gush there is most of all blather—useless or nearly useless words, images, and sounds that you nonetheless spend valuable time consuming, understanding, sorting, filing, and transmitting. In addition, the blather is often printed on paper—memos, journals, newspapers, briefs, flyers, forms, books, pamphlets, magazines—which creates the cousin of blather: clutter.

Blather and clutter fill so much of the gush that it is difficult to pick out the valuable nuggets buried within, like pearls in a pile of gravel. Piles of clutter proliferate—indeed, metastasize—through offices, while blather wafts from televisions, radios, cell phones, voice mails, and human conversations. The keen edge your mind had at the start of the day dulls as it tries to cut through the rubberous rind that surrounds blather and clutter.

I have seen people reduced to tears as they tell me of the clutter that fills their offices. They have even brought me photos to prove their point, doubting that I would believe how bad it is without hard evidence. These people, otherwise competent individuals, fall to their knees before their clutter, as if prayer were the only remedy left. When I ask them the obvious questions, like "Why don't you set aside time to clean up your office or hire someone else to do it for you?" they look at me as if I were a child, oblivious to the advanced nature of their disease.

These people have tried all the obvious cures, but they are still unable to get organized. Extreme but hardly rare, the problem is so common that there are 2,718 books listed on Amazon.com on the subject of getting organized and 300 devoted to the specific topic of clutter. That's nothing, though, compared with what a Google search finds. The term *getting organized* brings up 15,200,000 entries. When given the word *clutter*, Google brings up 4,620,000 entries, while *blather*, hardly a common word, gives you 816,000 Google replies.

Managing blather and clutter has become an industry that in its own right creates tons of blather and clutter. I have read many of the books. Most are full of blather and when stacked up create clutter. I have also met many of the "experts" on getting organized. While some are true geniuses, many are hopelessly disorganized themselves, trying to make a living by advising people not to make the mistakes they know about only too well.

Megatons of equipment and millions of acres of space go into storing clutter and blather. Filing cabinets, closets, attics, basements, crates, storage lockers, junk yards, bedroom floors, kitchen cabinets, purses, wallets, trunks of cars (not to mention floors and backseats), sheds, garages, warehouses, canisters, mattresses, cubbyholes, caverns, safes, barges, dumps, sewers, and all kinds of other receptacles and holding bins are bursting trying to contain the clutter that spews out of stores, houses, offices, labs, cars, factories, and so on every day. Garbology, the study of garbage and trash, is a discipline in which one can get a PhD. Indeed, I have a friend who is a professor of garbology at a large university. He fears that the world can't keep up with the demands for storing, eliminating, or safely sequestering the trash and garbage we will make upon it.

And how many trillion trillions of gigabytes of computer storage space are electronically preserving all the blather that we put into our electronic devices? Unsorted, truth mixed with fiction, Shakespeare mixed with phone records, this cyber storage bank is one of the greatest creations in the history of the world. But what in the world are we to do with it? How can anyone manage it? Still, it's a lot of fun trying.

Everywhere you go you must contend with blather or clutter or both. There's no escaping them. For example, I am writing this chapter on an airplane on my way home to Boston from Seattle. The cup of coffee I just drank had some writing on it. Being drawn to words wherever I see them, I read what was on the cup. Except for the names of the companies, here is what the cup said: "The bold, smooth taste of _____ coffee & the uncompromising service of _____ Airlines. It's no wonder we've become the perfect travel companions."

It wasn't bad enough that I read the words. Then I had to react to them. Bold taste? Blather. I drank the coffee, and believe me, it wasn't bold. And uncompromising service? What does that mean? Does it mean no one in the airline will ever compromise with a customer, but rather will behave like the inflexible bureaucrats that have made so many airlines unpopular? Finally, to what does the "we've" refer? The coffee and the airline? Do the writers mean to animate the coffee and the airline into a "we," as if the coffee and the airline were human? Not only did I have to think all those annoyed thoughts, I also had to scold myself for being seduced, for giving the damn coffee cup's advertising the attention it sought but didn't deserve.

Blather and clutter so predominate the gush that we accept them without realizing what we're doing or putting up any resistance. Advertising is everywhere, slipped into movies now, intruding onto our telephone lines, plastered throughout magazines and newspapers, and even inserted into them so that your morning paper or latest issue of *Time* often drops bits of advertising out of its pages as you pick them up, forcing you to take note of what you otherwise would ignore.

In a scene straight out of *1984*, I recently stood in an elevator in a large New York hotel in which the day's CNN broadcast blathered forth from a TV screen that couldn't be turned off. I said to the woman standing next to me as I pointed at the screen, "Don't you hate that we're forced to put up with this?"

"I've grown used to it," she replied glumly. Haven't we all?

Not only does blather intrude, we invite it in and even create it ourselves. Few people dare say what they mean. Human conversation has become more blather than not, as political correctness takes the flavor out of the meat and the inability to use simple words renders what many people say insipid and forgettable. Grunts would convey more meaning and punch than much of what passes for conversation today. Politicians have always specialized in blather, and they do so now more than ever. Blather has spread like a fungus to the point that it is impossible not to breathe it in every day, letting it infect our own minds.

15 Blind Baseball

Perhaps we live now in the storm before the calm. Or maybe the storm before the calamity. Who knows?

Passing through security at Logan Airport one June morning in 2005, I set off the alarm, as I always do because of the titanium shaft in my left femur (resulting from a total hip replacement). The agent who patted me down and wanded me for explosives started to guess my line of work while he did his otherwise boring job. "Lawyer? Doctor? Writer? Finance? Academics?"

I was surprised at his congeniality and intrigued by his reasoning. "I'm a doctor," I replied, "and a writer. How did you know?"

"I used to be in manufacturing until I got laid off a year ago when my job went to China. I figure jobs like mine have pretty much left this area. So what's left are doctors, lawyers, writers, finance, and the rest of you whose jobs can't be done cheaper in China."

"Is this job okay?" I asked optimistically.

"I'm fifty," he replied. "No one wants someone my age. It isn't pretty. This is the best I could find. I get paid fourteen dollars an hour. That's forty percent of what I used to make. And I have to commute all the way up here from New Bedford. At least an hour each way. I shouldn't complain, I've got my health and my family, but working security at Logan isn't the way I thought I'd end my career."

"You haven't lost your friendliness," I said.

"Give me time," the man replied with a chuckle.

"Oh, I doubt that you will," I said, trying to be encouraging but hearing the sadness and resignation in the man's words. As I walked on to my gate, I shuddered at what was happening to the world.

I'm fifty-five myself, more than halfway through my life, and my wife, Sue, is forty-nine. My kids, Lucy, Jack, and Tucker, are sixteen, thirteen, and ten. They are just at the beginning. I am optimistic by nature, but I find it difficult not to worry about what awaits my children and their children.

What jobs will be left for them? What condition will the world's environment be in when my kids grow up, and their kids? How much will the gap between the ultrarich and the rest of America damage our society? How will our current not-so-good reputation around the world create problems for our children and grandchildren?

Not being expert in any field that can analyze those questions intelligently, I simply worry about them, hoping that our leaders will address them before it's too late.

But the field that I am expert in—the workings of the mind—leads me to modern questions of a different sort, questions that I have been working on with my patients and mulling over myself for over twenty-five years. These are the questions of how modern life is affecting how we think, feel, and act, the questions I am taking up in this book.

The man at the security gate has had to adjust emotionally as well as economically. He's seen his hopes for his last years of work dashed. There are tens if not hundreds of thousands like him in this country alone, and the number is bound to increase as *billions* of workers from around the world compete for what used to be American jobs. That leads me, and many like me, to worry if we are doing all we can to make sure that that man's fate does not befall our children or us.

Just as busy describes us, so does worry. Statistics show anxiety disorders are on the rise. And those are just the diagnosable disorders. Toxic worry—worry beyond what is useful—runs rampant in America, and not just since 9/11. The surge in worry began before that, somewhere in the early nineties. By now the problem has hit childhood; ask any teacher or professional who deals with children regularly, and he or she will confirm what I have observed firsthand: Children are more worried today than any of us can remember their having been before.

This is not necessarily all bad, as extra worry accompanies all periods of change, change for the better as well as change for the worse. The lives of many people are changing for the better these days. The problem is, many of us do not yet know which group the future will usher us into or which group our children will eventually join. In this flat world, barriers of geography, time, class, and traditional loyalties have collapsed, allowing billions of people who used to be excluded from the race to riches to join in.

The waters of this new world are reequilibrating, as if the moon had changed its size, causing tides to rise to new highs and fall to new lows around the globe. Water is pouring in where it hasn't been for centuries, irrigating what used to be economic deserts—China and India in particular—while water is flowing away from other spots, drying up what used to be fertile crescents. New crescents are getting fertilized. These new ones depend not on the luck of geography, but rather on the taking advantage of new opportunities. Success depends upon mental agility, a desire and an ability to learn, adaptability, resilience, and creativity as much as hard work and sellable skills. We can't rest easy, at least not the 99 percent of us who aren't impregnably wealthy, and even those blessed souls who are must contend with the many miseries in life that are unrelated to money. As the man at Logan Airport painfully found out, the days of even remotely predictable futures are over.

Unless you are one of those people who believe that the final judgment is near and there is nothing we can do to stave it off, you—and I—need to think about how to play this new game.

Actually, the game is the same—getting on in life, pursuing happiness, realizing our dreams, and helping others to do the same—but the way it's played is new. We are now playing what I call "blind baseball." The players have blurry vision, and the field is in motion. The pitcher has to pitch to a moving batter and catcher he can't discern, while the batter has to dance a jig to stay in place while trying to hit a ball he can't see clearly. He must develop his other senses. If he is lucky—or adept—enough to hit the ball, he has to run to a base he can't quickly locate, while fielders try frantically to chase down a ball they can't quite see, using intuition, guile, and whatever else they can draw upon to get to the ball. If the players keep playing this confusing game, gradually their sight sharpens. Gradually they see that the field hasn't been moving at all; the movement was an illusion created by their poor vision. Gradually, they adapt. However, those who stayed fearfully on the sidelines remain in a blur on a field that still seems to move.

The blind time on an apparently moving field—which is

now—is frightening, albeit bracing, even thrilling. We can't follow old procedures because those depended on clear sight. For a certain kind of person, this is great news. At last, permission to throw out the old and invent the new. After all, we have to make up new ways to get on base. Irreverence, open-mindedness, people skills, creativity, intuition, the willingness to take a chance, fail, and still take another chance and another—these are valuable, along with luck. Working hard and working smart are, of course, vital, but even more vital is connecting with others so as not to give up in the face of confusion and uncertainty. And programming what you can program, predicting what you can predict, organizing what you can organize so that some of what you do will become automatic and you can find your rhythm, freeing your brain to use most of its neurons in the service of creative thinking.

Creating a positive emotional environment. Finding your rhythm. These are the keys.

It also helps if you like to play.

16 New Words for New Problems— Some with New Solutions

Gemmelsmerch. Screensucking. Gigaguilt. I have made up new words to describe some of the strangeness of modern life. Just as the automobile gave us terms like traffic jam, gridlock, and road rage, air travel terms like jet lag and holding pattern, our latest technologies are begetting their own new words or new uses for old words, like geek, boot up, fax, blog, e-mail, byte, RAM, Web site, and many more.

The new words and terms I have made up do not describe the technology itself; rather, these words and terms describe situations or emotions in need of a name owing to the circumstances of our lives today, circumstances brought on in part by our various technologies. Some of the emotions are not new—like guilt—but the modern representation has unique characteristics. I invented the word *gigaguilt* to describe what is new about guilt these days. Some are activities we have done for years, like watching TV, but the modern version of that activity has mushroomed into what I call "screensucking." One of the words is entirely nonsensical; I made it up to describe a force in nature that has no name, the force that distracts us from what we want to be doing. It didn't need a name until the current age because it was never as ubiquitous or dangerous as it is today. The name I gave I mentioned in the last chapter: "gemmelsmerch."

I also offer some ideas on how to deal with the problems each term describes. While some of the issues are timeless—like guilt—we need methods of dealing with the issues that are tailored to their modern manifestations. Others of the issues—like screensucking—are new and require not only methods of dealing with them, but also the raising of awareness that these issues exist and can cause big trouble.

Screensucking: Wasting time engaging with any screen—for instance, computer, video game, television, BlackBerry. Example: "I was supposed to write that article, but instead I spent the whole afternoon screensucking." Or, "I haven't finished my PhD dissertation mainly because I spend so much time screensucking, pretending that I'm doing actual research." Or, "I used to have a sex life, but now I spend all my nights screensucking, and by the time I get to bed my spouse is asleep."

Held by a mysterious force, a person can sit long after the work has been done or the show he wanted to watch is over, absently glommed on to the screen, not especially enjoying what he is doing but not able to disconnect and turn off the machine.

A kind of modern addiction, screensucking can create serious problems if it gets out of hand.

Screensucking is a difficult problem to solve, because it is done unintentionally. To combat it, you need to be aware that you are susceptible to it every time you log on or switch on. It's similar to drinking alcohol: Once you start, you need to be careful how much you consume. Insight can lead to moderation. If the problem becomes severe, you can put an alarm clock next to the device and set it to go off at the time you want to disconnect.

Leeches and **Lilies:** In modern life, your time and attention are more vulnerable to theft than ever before. Leeches are people or projects that waste your time and attention. They leave you feeling depleted and wondering why you ever got into this line of work, or this family, or this town. Lilies, on the other hand, are people or projects that, when you engage with them, make you feel fulfilled and satisfied, glad to be alive and doing what you're doing. It is a good idea to get rid of as many leeches as you can rather than try to complete them (in the case of projects) or make them happy (in the case of people). And it is a very good idea to cultivate your lilies to the fullest.

There are many reasons people have trouble getting rid of leeches. Habit is one. Guilt is another. Stubbornness is a third, and fear is a fourth. If you find that you are "friends" with someone who doesn't behave like a friend, there is no reason you can't distance yourself from her. Let her waste someone else's time or hurt someone else's feelings. Give yourself permission to make the most of the short time you have on this planet.

If you are stubbornly persisting in trying to make a failed project succeed, consider how much better you could spend your time. Too often people waste years trying to get good at what they're bad at instead of trying to do what they're good at.

If you are simply in the habit of tolerating leeches, wake up! Life is short. Don't let habit dictate what you do.

Doomdarts: Since most of us take on more than we can easily handle, it is especially difficult to keep track of everything. "Doomdart" is my word for an obligation you have forgotten about that suddenly pops into your consciousness like a poisoned dart. You may be cheerfully driving along in your car, or happily making dinner, or contentedly reading a book, when out of nowhere a forgotten obligation (your husband's birthday present, the review you promised your friend you would write of his proposal, the pledge you were supposed to pay but had successfully overlooked) pierces your consciousness and spreads its toxins throughout your being so that within minutes you are anxious and distracted.

The solution here is to make a plan in your mind of how you are going to take care of the problem as soon as the doomdart hits you. "I'll take care of it later" is not a plan. The doomdart will stay stuck, secreting its poisons. You need to tell yourself when and how you are going to take care of it, and your internal monitor needs to okay the plan. Then the dart will fall out and you can go on without pain.

EMV, or **e-mail voice:** The unearthly tone a person's voice takes on when he is reading e-mail while talking to you on the telephone. Although subtle, it is unmistakable. When you hear it you may choose to ignore it, tell the person to stop reading e-mail, or start reading e-mail yourself. There is an analogous voice when the person is watching television while talking to you, or reading the newspaper, or listening to a ball game on the radio.

Some clever people at the Massachusetts Institute of Technology's Media Lab have developed a program for monitoring your attention electronically as you speak on your cell phone. Called the "Jerk-O-Meter," the device is not yet precise and still sounds a bit tongue-in-cheek. But it is only a matter of time before more sophisticated devices can get implanted in electronics everywhere. Here's how the Associated Press reported on this, August 12, 2005:

> Researchers at the Massachusetts Institute of Technology are developing software for cell phones that would analyze

speech patterns and voice tones to rate people—on a scale of 0 to 100 percent—on how engaged they are in a conversation.

Anmol Madan, who led the project while he pursued a master's degree at MIT, sees the Jerk-O-Meter as a tool for improving relationships, not ending them. Or it might assist telephone sales and marketing efforts.

"Think of a situation where you could actually prevent an argument," he said. "Just having this device can make people more attentive because they know they're being monitored."

The program, which Madan said is nearing completion, uses mathematical algorithms to measure levels of stress and empathy in a person's voice. It also keeps track of how often someone is speaking.

Most people do not need a Jerk-O-Meter to know if they are paying attention or if the person on the other end of the line is. EMV is detectable to the naked ear, as it were.

The remedy for EMV is to point it out when it happens. It is a symptom of a busy life. While rude, it is so common as to be routine. If you do not want a person to talk to you while doing something else, point it out gently. That should be enough to bring the person back. If you yourself are doing it, consider how annoying it is when it is done to you. On the other hand, you can simply talk to someone else who is simultaneously doing e-mail.

Gigaguilt: Computer technology and its gigabytes of memory have directly and indirectly so extended the number of items a person must keep track of (finite, large number), not to mention *can expect himself* to keep track of (huge, practically infinite number), that the likelihood of missing something has skyrocketed. It is a 100 percent likelihood for most of us. This brings with it guilt, lots of guilt, ceaseless guilt, guilt in the morning, guilt in the evening, guilt all the day long. "Gigaguilt" refers to this guilt, the guilt a person feels over missing something or disappointing someone, even while knowing that keeping track of *everything* is impossible and having enough time to please *everyone* is equally impossible.

Guilt over not having done enough is hardly new. In the seventeenth century, John Milton reminded us and himself, "They also serve who only stand and wait," as he felt guilty over his declining powers owing to his blindness. In the eighteenth century, that brilliant paragon of guilt Samuel Johnson tried to reassure himself—and us—that "no man is obliged to do as much as he can do." What is new, however, are the gigabytes, which have extended the possibilities of guilt beyond what even the devil might have hoped for.

Like so many painful emotions, gigaguilt does not respond well to reason. It is unreasonable to expect the impossible of yourself, yet many of us feel guilty when we do not achieve the impossible, even though we know full well it is impossible to do the impossible.

The best remedy for gigaguilt that I know of is to supplement reason with structure. Set limits on what you commit to. Reserve time for what matters most to you, and if you feel guilty that you are not serving others when you are doing what matters most to you, remind yourself that you would be of much less use to others if you did not do what matters most to you some of the time. You would become depressed, frazzled, impatient, resentful, and ineffective.

Also, have a system that can dictate for you what you will commit to and what you won't. For example, you can make it a policy that you will serve on only one volunteer committee at a time. Or you can make it a policy that you will take on only a certain number of clients or patients or customers at a time. Don't take calls during dinner. Set a regular time that you call your mother so you don't have to feel guilty the rest of the time and so that she can depend on getting your call. In general, develop a system for dealing with all the demands on your time that come up regularly so you don't have to decide on the spot each time.

Finally, have a talk with yourself, or with someone else, to get settled with the fact that you cannot do everything for everybody or even do as much for others as you might like to do.

Gigaguilt itself is inevitable, given a certain kind of personality—that is, being a nice person. How much you let gigaguilt run your life is what you *do*, in fact, have some control over.

Taildogging: Going faster or pushing harder—on yourself, your children, your business, your spouse—simply because other people are doing so. Allowing the tail to wag the dog, you take on more than you want to for yourself, for your children, or for others mostly out of fear that if you don't, you—or your children, family, or business—will be left behind in life's great race. People buy into myths en masse, myths like: that a child having an expensive computer leads to success in school, or that driving a Mercedes is good for the soul, or that being a member of a club you don't enjoy will somehow enhance your life, or that having a swimming pool is one of life's necessities, or that an outrageously expensive, lavish birthday party for a seven-year-old is de rigueur. These myths are the tails that wag the dogs, our lives. How many people do you know who are planning a birthday party they can't afford simply because one of their children's friends had such a party?

While this phenomenon, what I call "taildogging," has

always been a part of life, the social disconnection that is such a part of modern culture has weakened the ties we have with others to such an extent that we are unable to get and give the reassurances that would prevent us from doing the outrageous, in an effort to keep up with what is unnecessary, in the first place.

The solution to this problem in the long run is to restore connectedness to our culture. In the meantime, a person must have the courage of her convictions and not buy the presents just because someone else does, not get the SAT tutoring when it isn't needed just because someone else does.

Kudzu: A weed inadvertently imported into the United States from Southeast Asia. Once it takes root, it spreads like proverbial wildfire, invading acre upon acre. Once in place, it is all but unkillable. It sends down roots of one hundred feet or more, great pinkish-orange roots that look like giant squid tentacles out of a horror movie. For the purposes of this book, "kudzu" is the term I apply to the clutter and piles that invade where we work and where we live, the unstoppable, unkillable stream of unexpected minor requests from people everywhere that slow us down, the spam that infests our e-mail, the junk mail that overruns our snail mail, and the useless information that we continue to collect in spite of our best efforts not to.

One of the great antidotes to physical kudzu is the acronym OHIO: only handle it once. When it comes to a document or journal or any concrete item, try your best to 1) respond to it right away, 2) put it in a labeled file, not a pile, or 3) throw it away. In the majority of instances, choice "3" is the best.

As for the requests that stream in from everywhere, the best antidote is a blockade. Don't let them reach you. What you haven't heard you can't feel guilty about not doing. You can create blockades in whatever fashion that suits you. Just don't keep your door open to everyone. This was a nice idea at one time in history, say, even a decade ago. Now it is like opening your door to the Hoover Dam.

Gemmelsmerch: Gemmelsmerch is even more dangerous than kudzu. As I mentioned in chapter 13, this is my word for the force that distracts the mind or steals it away from what it wants to do or ought to be doing. The word has no meaning or root that I know of; I just wanted to make up a complicated-sounding, sticky word to describe this complicated, sticky force. Accidents along the highway are high in gemmelsmerch, compelling drivers to slow down and gawk. A jackhammer outside your window is high in gemmelsmerch. Getting news that you will be audited by the IRS is high in gemmelsmerch. Television shows—or almost anything that appears on a screen—are high in gemmelsmerch; screens exert a mysterious magnetism upon the human eyeball that science has yet to explain. Angry rants on the radio are high in gemmelsmerch. Sex and violence of all kinds are high in gemmelsmerch. As if covered in a radioactive cloud of the stuff, the world has never been as high in gemmelsmerch as it is today. Reducing gemmelsmerch in your environment and learning how to resist its pull are modern survival skills of the highest importance.

For solutions to gemmelsmerch, see chapter 28.

Morning Burst: The time of day when you are mentally at your freshest, most able to concentrate and think clearly, least burdened by annoyances and new tasks, most able to bring your entire mind to bear on a single task. For most people this is in the morning, hence the name. For some people, however, it comes at midday or even in the evening. In modern life, it is important to know when your morning burst comes and to make sure you use that time to full advantage, doing your most important, most difficult work.

Morning Bust: What your morning burst can turn into if you don't protect that time from intrusions.

Junk Time: The time-stealing equivalent of Doritos. I stole this term from the food world to describe the many activities we can gorge on before we get to the main task, leaving little room for it. For example, a person can sit down at her desk fully intending to compose the important memo that needs to be sent out soon. When her computer boots up, instead of going straight to her word-processing program, she checks in first with her e-mail and ends up staying there for forty-five minutes. E-mail is a classic consumer of junk time. A person can spend oodles of it without intending to, leaving insufficient time for what really needs to get done. Other dangerous consumers of junk time include the cell phone, voice mail, instant messaging, the newspaper, long-winded people, magazines (*People* is the most notorious), CNN, television in general, or the colleague who sticks his head in your door and says, "I don't mean to interrupt you, but . . ."

Telephone Tag: An annoying but well-known phenomenon that is becoming obsolete as more and more people carry cell phones and BlackBerrys.

Conversation Interruptus: While conversations have been interrupted throughout history, they are interrupted so frequently now that an extended conversation is becoming as rare as a three-martini lunch. Indeed, it may take three martinis for you to ignore the many signals that vie for your attention and conspire to interrupt your every conversation.

Pile-on: The phenomenon of your boss, your spouse, your children, their teachers, or simply fate piling task after task upon you, as if your capacity to handle them were limitless. Try to get in the habit of saying, "Stop!" or, "Enough!" before you become so desperate that you assault the next person who asks you to do something.

Info Addict: While there have always been people who crave information, there has never before been so much information so readily available. A person can consume information all day from a variety of sources—CNN, the Internet, newspapers, radio, even those relics called books—and feel starved when the information stops. Wanting what's new, what's the latest, what's now, a person can become all but addicted to keeping up, second to second, with what's "going on," relying totally on the judgment of others to select what belongs under that curious term. After a while, nothing goes on in the information addict's life except what others have decided is going on in the world.

In another of the many paradoxes of modern life, the info addict loses his or her own ability to make a difference in life by trying so hard to keep up with all the differences other people are making.

The Human Moment vs. **the Electronic Moment:** A human moment occurs when two or more people meet in person and connect with one another. If you are milling around in a shopping mall surrounded by other people, that is not a human moment, as you are not in connection with the others in the mall. An electronic moment occurs when you meet others via electronic devices such as the telephone, cell phone, e-mail, or fax. Over the past decade, human moments have increasingly been replaced by electronic moments. People spend less time in one another's physical presence. Family dinners, face-to-face conversations, and live meetings have been replaced by eating alone, by conversing on the cell phone or by IM, and by teleconferences.

The electronic moment is hugely efficient, rapid, and easy. However, the human moment conveys far more information: tone of voice, body language, facial expression, and all the nonverbal cues that constitute such a vital part of human communication. The electronic moment is great for the transmission of data. The more emotion that enters into the picture, the better it is to have a human moment.

Electronic Time: Time spent on electronic devices, including television, computers, the Net, e-mail, cell phone, BlackBerry, iPod, Game Boy, and the like. Too much electronic time and not enough human moments lead to an as yet unnamed medical condition, the symptoms of which are loss of personal vitality, the inability to converse, a craving for a screen when separated from one, and low-grade depression.

Frazzing: Multitasking ineffectively. Multitasking is a term that originated in computer engineering. It is what a computer does during the microseconds between keystrokes as you are typing. Humans adopted the term to mean doing several tasks simultaneously. For most people, multitasking is exciting, sometimes necessary, but rarely as efficient or effective as devoting your full attention to one task.

What most of us do is fraz. We multitask, hurriedly believing we are listening, writing, and reading all at the same time. In fact, we are switching our attention from one to the other so quickly that all activities seem to be happening simultaneously. But they are not. Furthermore, the quality of each is not as high as if we were doing one at a time.

There is a qualification I should make to this that I have learned from the world of ADD. Sometimes a person, myself included, can do better work when provided with some extraneous sensory input, such as music. Some kids actually do better homework while watching television. If you look closely, you will see they are not watching TV so much as enjoying the company of the TV. Lest you deceive yourself, you can do the experiment: Check the quality of your work with music and the quality without.

I once worked with a man who did his best writing standing up. Something about the sensory stimulation of standing helped focus his mind. Indeed, Thomas Wolfe wrote most of his novels standing up. He had a very high desk.

Pizzled: A combination of pissed-off and puzzled, "pizzled" denotes how you feel when a person, without either asking permission or providing an explanation, brings out his or her cell phone to make a call or answer a call while you are walking together, eating together, meeting together, riding together, or doing anything else together. A variant of the same emotion arises when a person at an adjacent table, booth, or seat does the same thing. As pizzle mounts, rage may ensue.

As modern life evolves, we will develop a new etiquette for such situations, but it is not clear what that will be. On the one hand, it may become as impolite to take a call on your cell when you are with someone as it would be to light up a cigarette in church. Or expedience may rule, and it will become polite to fall silent and wait while your companion takes care of the important business the cell phone or BlackBerry is bringing in.

The Spray Effect: This is what can happen to your attention if you are not careful. There is so much you must do each day, and on top of that so much you could do, that your attention can be splayed and head off in many directions at once, like water from a garden hose, whose nozzle has been set on wide spray. Instead, it is best to set your nozzle on jet stream. Focus your attention in one direction with full force so you can tackle one problem or take advantage of one opportunity without diluting your effort and frazzing.

The Megaloctopus: This beast pursues you every day. Wherever you go, the megaloctopus extends its tentacles, trying to trap you and keep you from doing what you're trying to do. The megaloctopus is made up of all the people who want your time, all the tasks you're supposed to get done, all the places you're supposed to go, all the opportunities you possibly could pursue, all the temptations you try to resist, all the hopes you've ever had as well as all the fears—in short, all that may rise up and steal you away from the task you are trying to complete right now, in the present moment.

The best way to combat the megaloctopus is to know it's there. Don't fall into the trap of believing you ought to do everything you're asked to do or could do. The megaloctopus depends upon your believing that. You can do only what you can do, and you will do what you can do much more effectively if you're not trying frantically to squeeze in more than you reasonably can. Cut those tentacles when they start to entwine you.

Fuhgeddomania and **Loseophilia:** While people have always struggled with the problems of forgetfulness and losing things, today's rush and gush have made these problems make millions believe they have early Alzheimer's. People are flocking to doctor's offices to make sure they do not have some kind of dementia, as they swear that their memory is fading fast and they can't keep track of items as well as they used to.

"Fuhgeddomania" and "Loseophilia" denote the modern manifestations of these age-old problems. The amount of data and items people have to remember and organize today exceeds what it has ever been before in history. What looks like forgetfulness derived from a neurological problem is really fuhgeddomania, forgetfulness derived from data overload. And what looks like a tendency to lose things based on some kind of brain decay is really loseophilia, a tendency to lose things based on the fact that a person has more things to keep track of than a normal human brain can manage.

The solutions to both fuhgeddomania and loseophilia are to add structure to the environment—lists, reminders, filing systems, computer programs—and to delegate the tasks of remembering and organizing whenever possible. Placing certain items in the same place every time you finish using them helps combat the problem of loseophilia. In addition, it is good to set a limit on how much you commit yourself to remembering or keeping track of.

Fast: A modern synonym for good. How good depends upon how fast.

Slow: A synonym for agonizing (if really slow), boring (if just ordinarily slow), or of poor quality (if merely lacking in speed). For instance, a date that was slow could have been agonizing or boring. Same with a movie, a book, a day, a job, a weekend, or a conversation. One sign of age is that slow slowly loses its negative meanings.

17 An Alphabet of Reasons Why We Are So Busy

"Is it normal," one of my patients asked me in all sincerity, "that my husband lays his BlackBerry down next to us when we make love?" That this woman had any doubt whatsoever that her husband's behavior was unacceptable, if not insane, was the moment when I knew for sure that we had created a new world. When receiving and sending messages could assume such high priority that nothing, not even making love, could stand in the way; and when an intimate partner could doubt herself for feeling upset at the intrusion of the BlackBerry into the bedroom, then I knew that our new world had gone mad in its addiction to messages.

There are times when we need to shut down the BlackBerry and give the other person our total attention, face to face. Making love would seem to be such a time, but there are many others. Whenever emotion matters, whenever subtlety counts, whenever the issues are complex and in need of explanation, or the content is joyful and in need of celebration—these are just some of the times when it's best that we are there in person, without distractions.

Instead, we too often allow ourselves to fall under the mysteriously addicting spell of the screen and its seductive messaging, denying ourselves the far richer and more fulfilling human moment of in-person interaction.

BlackBerry and the many other creators and manufacturers of similar handheld miracles of technology proudly trumpet their products' ability to provide users with instant access to anyone, anywhere, anytime in various modes: voice, type, or image. Amazing. We can send and receive messages while doing just about anything else anywhere else.

We can feel compelled to log on, to boot up, to download. Like addicts, we can itch and scratch and pace and fuss until we get our fix. We've discovered a new addiction with enormous appeal and power. Don't we all have a bit of the BlackBerry addict in us? And don't we increasingly find these Pilots and Berrys irresistible?

On the other hand (and in case you haven't noticed, I think modern life is all about "other hands," paradoxes and complexities galore), when you consider the "advantages" of a BlackBerry and crave them as if they were an orgasmic array, imagining yourself able to be everywhere and do everything 24/7/365, you may feel excited, but don't you also feel slightly ill? "I can be in touch anywhere" is just one crazybusy moment away from, "I *must* be in touch *everywhere*."

It is indeed wonderful to be able to use your BlackBerry, cell phone, or laptop anywhere, while you wait. I do it all the time myself. For the unwary, and there are millions, it can feel like such a compelling opportunity that it becomes a true addiction. But you might wonder, What does it take the place of? What did we do, say, in airports while waiting for our flights before we had BlackBerrys, cell phones, and laptops? Veg out? Talk on pay phones? Read? Think? Sleep? Daydream? Entertain new ideas? Converse with other people in person? Eat? Drink? Be merry?

Not likely the last one very often, but all the others for sure. How marvelous to be able to turn wasted waiting time into productive time. Right?

But watch out. It is marvelous only as long as you remain in charge instead of letting the technology take charge of you. Our current ability to bring our offices and all our contacts with us wherever we go transforms wherever we go into a place where we always are. The physical surroundings matter less and less. We live by fielding more and more messages, processing more and more data points, while rushing to the ubiquitous trough to get still more. When do we stop and think? When do we linger over a thought? When do we make love?

If we're not careful, we start reading and sending messages everywhere we go. At lunch with a friend, while waiting in traffic, or perhaps while getting a colonoscopy. Why not?

There's no stopping this electronic world now, nor should we want to stop it. It is spectacular and it drives much of our prosperity. We are accomplishing great things these days. We are increasingly free from offices and wires and boring meetings or down time.

But I wonder, What is the tickle? What is the itch these electronic devices scratch? Why do so many of us crave being in constant touch everywhere and always? What is in these thousands of messages that is so important? Why can't they wait? They always used to. Why do we allow ourselves to become crazybusy, keeping up with the latest information, the most recent news flash, the latest stock quote, the most recent e-mail, instead of putting our feet up and reading a good book, thinking a long thought, enjoying a lasting kiss, or just staring out the window for a minute or two?

Of course, most messages *can* wait, and we often let them

do just that. Our machines receive email 24/7/365, and many programs can sort them for us, even alert us when certain ones appear. But no one answers e-mail 24/7/365. We still are usually sane enough to make messages wait to be heard or read.

On the other hand, we act as if we will go into withdrawal if we can't log on or dial. When the plane lands, cell phones pop open and BlackBerrys get powered up. A sort of feeding frenzy takes over the airplane as passengers who had been e-mail-deprived for the length of the trip can log on. No one smokes anymore, but the old nicotine fit has been replaced by the fit to log on.

Why are we all so busy?

We keep so busy because:

a) *We can be.* Can you imagine how *bored* we must have been before we had cell phones and e-mail?

b) *We want to be.* Nothing quite matches the excitement of checking e-mail every ten minutes or checking a stock price sixty-five times in a day.

c) *We must be.* The wolf is at the door. It is named China. The wolf behind it is named India. Third in line is the guy down the street.

d) *We* imagine *that we must be.* All the smart people say that life is really insecure these days so we better stay busy to get ready for the bad times ahead.

e) *Busy is fun.* Speed is the modern natural high. (Not the drug speed, but the feeling you get from going fast.)

f) *We let too many leeches into our lives.* (See previous chapter for definition of leech.)

g) *We overcommit.* Do you know anyone who doesn't?

h) *Others overcommit us.* Wouldn't you like to be one of those tough people who can actually say no and stick to it?

i) *We let our technology run us instead of us running our technology* (cell phone, BlackBerry, computer, e-mail, voice mail, Internet, and so on). Hal from the movie *2001: A Space Odyssey* is chuckling as he watches us all running to keep up with his offspring.

j) *We work hard but not smart.* Again, "work smart" is common advice. Hardly a revelation. No one tries to work stupid. So why do we? For the same reason we won't listen when someone offers us a shorter route from here to there.

k) *Being busy is a status symbol.* Isn't that strange?

l) *We are afraid of being left out or missing something if we slow down.* This is taildogging, as defined in the previous chapter.

m) *We are afraid that we will not keep up our standard of living unless we are superbusy.* More taildogging.

n) *We can avoid the pain of life.* You know, like the abyss, meaninglessness, gratuitous human cruelty, death, world hunger, global warming, AIDS, the nuclear threat, terrorism, and all the other problems we don't know how to deal with.

o) *We can avoid everything that is difficult that we don't want to do.* Like following that dream we keep putting off. Or helping our child with physics homework.

p) *We don't have to feel guilty about doing nothing.* And still we manage to feel guilty!

q) *Someone in our lives convinced us that the devil finds work for idle hands.* Don't you just hate those aphorisms we grew up with? My most unfavorite is "Trifles make perfection, and perfection is no trifle."

r) *Everyone else is busy.* Therefore, being busy must be the right thing to do. Monkey see, monkey do. Welcome to our zoo.

s) *You have an excuse* not to go to parties you don't want to go to; visit people you don't want to visit; serve on boards or committees you don't want to serve on; or explain to your neighbor why you haven't invited him and his insufferable den of conniving, superficial materialists over for a barbecue; not to mention see that relative whose politics make you want to punch him out.

t) *You're not bored when you're busy.* Actor George Sanders left an infamous suicide note in which he said that he was leaving the world because he was bored. However, I think it is possible to be both busy *and* bored.

u) *You don't have to think too much.* What a relief!

v) *Being busy is better than not knowing what to do.*

w) *You believe that being busy is the best way to get to where you want to go.*

x) *You're trying to create time when you won't have to be busy.*

y) *You don't know how not to be busy.*

z) *All of the above.*

If you answered *z*, I agree with you.

18 Why Women Have It Harder Than Men

Take my wife, Sue, as an example. She works part-time as a psychotherapist while organizing the lives of our three children and taking care of our home "part-time." It is a huge task. Every day I marvel at how she plans her day, like an air traffic controller managing continual incoming and outgoing flights; only the flights Sue must control often come in unannounced. What to do about the essential notebook that was left at school Friday and now it's Sunday afternoon and time to do the assignment? Which kid needs to be picked up when and where? Whose day is it for carpooling? When is lacrosse practice? When is the dentist appointment? Who can bring Tucker the violin that he left at home? What can she make for dinner tonight? What's on sale? To whom can she refer the patient she saw yesterday for a medication evaluation? Are there any new messages on voice mail? When can she grab a moment to check e-mail? Is there time to get to the gym? What about lunch? Did Lucy put her laundry in or are we going to have a big fight about that tonight? How can she explain to Jack's coach that he would do much better playing another position without her coming across like a pushy mom? Is her book group this week or next? Will there be time to pick up Lucy before Tucker needs to be picked up or should she get him first and keep Lucy waiting? Is Ned [me] flying out tomorrow or the next day, and when does he get back? And who is going to take care of the kids if he doesn't get back until Thursday? . . . all deliberations that can be interrupted, and usually are, by the cell phone ringing to tell her a sick child needs to be picked up at school or a friend of one of the kids wants to have a sleepover or one of her patients is in a crisis.

Sue does have a maximum, but it is very high. Nonetheless, she does reach it, and when she does, mistakes happen. They are usually little mistakes—Sue has never left a baby in a car seat on the roof of the car as she drove away or set the house on fire by forgetting to shut off a burner on the stove—but the little mistakes upset her to no end, as her standards are unforgivingly high. She gets angry at herself, angry at others (like me), and loses track of what's going on, but she is more adept at righting herself than anyone I know. It always amazes me that she gets done what she does get done. But it also amazes me how much more she does—exponentially more—than, say, my mother did.

This is the life of the modern working mom. It is also the life of the working dad who has assumed responsibility for most of the child care and housework, but in general it is a woman who is both the primary caretaker and a wage earner. There she stands, tending the grill, organizing dozens of orders, and always ready for sudden requests from the counter behind.

19 Not Your Father's Oldsmobile—or Toyota

For the working man or working woman without children, life is also high speed and rat-a-tat-tat. It's easier for a working dad (like me, for example) than it is for a working mom (like my wife, for example), but the principle persists. I don't have as many, varied demands upon my time as Sue does, but I still have more than I would have had twenty-five years ago and far more than my father ever had. That's simply because now I have a cell phone (a Trēo or a BlackBerry is inevitably in my future), a laptop, a Web site, an e-mail address, a fax machine, and a FedEx account, none of which I had twenty-five years ago when I started out in my career. My father died before such a life was even imaginable.

I check my e-mail every day, usually several times a day; I check my voice mail at least twice a day, usually more; I am given messages by my office staff all the time; I carry my cell phone with me; and I have a fax machine both in my office and at home. I am always available. I like it like this. I get a lot done. Life is exciting.

But it is torture when my grill gets too full. When *too* many messages ask me to do *too* many things, when I have to furiously finish a column that is past due *and* prepare a lecture for the next day *and* respond to an urgent request from a patient—*and* call the insurance company about the tree I backed up into because I was in such a hurry—then I become nasty, irascible, impatient, inefficient, and a boor.

Having essentially three careers—writer, lecturer, and psychiatrist—as well as three other major life roles—father, husband, and friend—I have learned to balance many obligations and carry a lengthy to-do list in my mind, as have millions of others. My list balloons when I think about it, which is why I try not to think about it.

Like most people these days, I am busy, and I wouldn't have it any other way. As I did so many years ago, I try to spot the moment of overload. There is a brief interlude between the onset of overload and the development of spastic behavior during which I have the chance to back away from all that I am doing and regroup. If I can catch myself during that interlude—it lasts between a few seconds and a minute or two, depending upon the pressure of the situation and the volume of the demands—then I can save the rest of the day. Otherwise, I am shot. I will be grumpy and inefficient for the rest of the day, performing at a substandard level.

I call the first state, the one of effective performance and even temper, "C-state" (calm, cool, collected, and other words that begin with *c*). I call the other state, the one of inefficient performance and ill temper, "F-state" (frenzied, feckless, flustered, and other words that begin with *f*). Those two states are separated by the precious interlude of warning. To acquire the skill of identifying the interlude when you're in it, all you have to do is know that it exists and then listen to what your mind and body tell you. During the interlude, if you listen, you will hear yourself telling yourself, *You are about to lose it. Don't take the bait. Back away. Go outside. Take a break.* Listening to that voice can save a career, a marriage, or at least a day.

20 C-State and F-State

C-state is clear, calm, cool, collected, consistent, concentrated, convivial, careful, curious, creative, courteous, and coordinated. On the other hand, F-state fractures focus and is frenzied, feckless, flailing, fearful, forgetful, flustered, furious, fractious, feverish, and frantic. It can also drive one to utter the famous f-word. In C-state you have found your rhythm. In F-state you have lost it.

It is easy to move from C-state to F-state. For example:

It is midnight in New York. Jeff sits alone in his office. He is finishing up a proposal he had intended to write during the day, but, well, stuff got in his way.

First, he was buttonholed as he came in that morning by his boss, who asked him to participate in a conference call to Germany that ended up taking two full hours. No concern was expressed and no allowance was made for how this might upset his day. He was simply left with having to get more work done than there was time to do it in, at least at his ordinary, already brisk pace. So he started to sprint. He tore through his e-mails like a backhoe, gouging out words and whole sentences, clawing to get the bare essentials before moving to the next e-mail, responding only when absolutely necessary, tagging some to be dealt with later (but *when?*), pounding the keys on his keyboard as if they were stuck rocks, biting his tongue, pursing his lips, uttering various curses under his breath, becoming both angry and over-whelmed at the multitude of requests the e-mails disgorged, while in the back of his mind feverishly resenting that his boss had dragged him into the conference call without the least concern for the rest of his day.

Once through the e-mails—flagging dozens he would need to tend to before the day was over—he started to work on the proposal he had to deliver the next day. Ten minutes into that task, an important client called and said he was e-mailing Jeff a memo upon which he needed his opinion right away because the material was highly time-sensitive. Downloading the memo, Jeff looked aghast at its length as the little blue bar on the screen took forever to fill and complete. How was he going to pore over all that and give a responsible opinion "right away"?

Turning from a modern Jimmy Olsen into SuperExec, Jeff squinted and furrowed into hyperfocus mode. He asked Kelly, his assistant, to bring him a triple—three shots of espresso with milk. Knowing the drill all too well, she tried to speak some calming words when she delivered the infamous triple. It usually portended a bad day.

The memo was complicated. Still, Jeff thought he could find a way to compose a reasonable answer. But was it a $600-per-hour answer, an answer he would be confident enough about to put in writing and attach his name and the firm's to? Tension mounted in his forebrain as he absently scratched the back of his neck, gulped his caffeine, and rapidly tapped his pencil on the leather border of his blotter. Finally, biting his lip, he took the plunge and put fingers to keyboard to draft a reply. A paragraph into it, he stopped without knowing he'd stopped and stared at a blank piece of paper to the left of his keyboard, doodling on it with his pencil as he did so. When he snapped out of his daydream, he looked down and noticed that he had doodled in ornate script the word DOOM.

Flustered and unable to clear his mind, he went back online to recheck his e-mail. Intending to spend just a few minutes on this to give himself a breather, he instead spent an hour. Kelly then interrupted him to inform him that Dagmar Fitch had arrived for her appointment. Cursing the keyboard, Jeff stood up and went out to meet his client.

That meeting chewed up two more hours. Dagmar loved to talk, and Jeff couldn't cut her off. In the current climate, it was imperative to keep clients happy, especially wealthy ones like her. At least the two hours were billable.

After he bade farewell to Dagmar, giving her shoulder a confident, reassuring pat, he went back to the memo, all too aware that tomorrow's proposal waited silently like a fiend, as yet untended to. There was no time to spare on fine points in the memo, so he composed an opinion as best he could and e-mailed it back to his client with a note: "Sorry this took longer than expected." Total turnaround time had been four hours. And he was sorry? That's the practice of law in modern life. Life had been so much easier when opinions had to be mailed or messengered; at least then there was a cutoff time beyond which the messenger would not come, at which point delivery had to wait until the next day—which meant completing it could wait as well.

Just as he was settling back to attack the proposal, a junior associate popped in with a complex question that a senior partner had declared Jeff—and only Jeff—should answer. Of course, it had to be answered right away. Jeff begged off, saying it would simply have to wait until tomorrow; but after the junior associate left his office, the guilt in Jeff rose to such a pitch that he cursed again, called the junior associate back, and turned his attention to the question. The kid was right, it was complex, but two hours later Jeff called the junior associate and gave him his answer.

By now the day was totally shot. He had not written one page of the proposal. Kelly was cheerfully packing up to go home as Jeff looked longingly not at her body but at her job. Wouldn't it be nice? And why not? Not bothering with the all too obvious answers to that last question (money, power, advancement, intellectual stimulation, prestige, destiny, upbringing, lack of alternatives, the horse having left the barn . . .), Jeff sighed and got back to work.

He was in F-state state now, distracted by all that had happened that day, annoyed at how his time had been stolen, irritated with himself for being pushed around so easily, but at the same time knowing he had to be flexible to do his job. His mind ricocheted from the proposal to these other concerns and *boing*ed back again like a ball in a pinball machine. Anxious that he couldn't get the proposal done in time, fearful of what that would mean, determined somehow to do it, angry that he was in this position, he kept working, his efficiency about one-quarter of what it normally would be.

His focus fracturing like a crack spreading through ice, he found it increasingly difficult to keep his mind on the proposal for any significant length of time. He had to keep pulling his attention back to the computer screen as if redirecting a somnambulist. Sleepwalking through the proposal, no longer efficient, he strained with his last few neurons of useful brainpower to somehow keep on task. He was on automatic pilot, propelled by ancient instincts of survival. By daybreak, miraculously, the proposal was done.

Welcome to our overloaded world, in which time and attention can be depleted before the day's work has even begun. Welcome to F-state.

As I mentioned earlier, F-state resembles attention deficit disorder. In ADD, the brain races and can't stop owing to its genetically set wiring. The chief problem with this race car brain is that its brakes do not work well. It's got a Ferrari engine but Chevrolet brakes. It can win races if it develops adequate brakes, but it will crash and burn if it doesn't.

The challenge of modern life, even for people who do not have ADD, is to learn how to put on the brakes. In order to cope with the many demands of everyday life and the information overload each day brings, a person needs to be able to stop and think, to pause over one point long enough to extract what matters before moving on. Otherwise the day becomes a blur in which no significant work gets done. Lots of energy gets expended, but it is mere sound and fury. In order for the energy to get focused, a person must be able to put the brakes on incoming stimuli and outgoing impulses long enough to concoct a complex thought. Life is a powerful accelerator these days; what separates the successful from the frustrated is the quality of their brakes and their ability to use them. As mentioned earlier, a summary of the symptoms of true ADD looks like a description of what many millions of Americans contend with today even if they do not have true ADD.

The similarities between the F-state so common in modern life and true ADD stand out when you look at this summary of the symptoms of true ADD:

- Difficulty focusing attention for more than a few seconds, tendency to tune out in the middle of a conversation, a meeting, or while reading a page, coupled with an ability to superfocus attention in a crisis or when imaginatively engaged in the project, topic, or conversation. The problem of inconsistent focus gets worse if the individual has not had enough sleep, has had only coffee and a Danish for breakfast (or no breakfast at all), has not exercised in the past forty-eight hours, and got hassled in traffic on the way in to work.
- Tendency to be restless, constantly in motion, physically or mentally or both.
- Tendency to have many projects going at once, trouble with follow-through, and even just keeping track of them all.
- Increasing irritability as the day goes on; increasingly poor tolerance of frustration.
- Labile moods. "Labile" is a term from chemistry that refers to a substance that can change quickly from one state to another, as from solid to liquid or liquid to gas. Labile moods are moods that can change quickly, as from agreeable to angry or from confident to anxious.
- Tendency always to feel in a rush; impatient.
- Tendency to want to cut to the chase or get to the bottom line immediately, even if this means bringing premature closure on discussion or explanation.
- A feeling of being overwhelmed by daily life, even when there isn't too much to do. Sometimes a feeling of being defeated even before you start.
- Difficulty in observing oneself, which leads to an inability to assess accurately how others are perceiving you.
- Trouble getting organized. Tendency to organize by placing things in piles. Getting organized means straightening up

your piles. The piles spread, like a tumor that is metastasizing, invading all parts of offices and homes, even extending out into the yard and onto the street.

• Trouble with time management. Tendency to procrastinate. The busier you get, the less sense of time you feel, so that pretty soon there are only two times in your mind: *now* and *not now*. You try desperately to put as much as you can into the "pile" of *not now*.

• Tendency to worry easily, even when there is no danger at hand, coupled with a tendency not to worry enough when real danger does lurk nearby. Hence the paradoxical tendency to live both in a world of exaggerated danger and in a world of denial or minimization.

• A chronic desire to alter your mental state, whether through fantasies of escape, or the use of alcohol or drugs, or impulsive gambling, sexualizing, eating, spending, or other means of scratching an itch that seems impossible to scratch.

• A chronic feeling of underachievement, of not reaching your goals, even though you may be achieving at a very high level indeed. This is because you know, if only you could find the key, that you could do much more and could be much happier. (The elusive key is learning how to manage your world and your brain instead of letting both of those manage you.)

• A tendency to be easily bored, coupled with an absolute, almost visceral intolerance of boredom. Unless bits of stimulation hit your brain every moment, you are liable to get bored and tune out.

• A constant search for high stimulation: action, noise, speed, the gush and the rush, conflict, sexual stimulation, breaking news, multitasking, bright colors, headlines, fame, association with fame, wealth, association with wealth, power, association with power, the bizarre, the strange, the forbidden. This craving of high stimulation is conditioned into the modern mind, while the person with ADD is born with it. Either way, the search for high stimulation is constant. The ability to linger or to wait atrophies. Harmony or contentment are too bland. You do not say someone was riveted in contentment. But a person can be riveted by conflict. However it happens, the modern mind demands it be riveted.

- A tendency to deal with difficulty by working harder rather than smarter.
- Owing to disorganization, frustration, and the feeling of being overloaded, the person tends to waste his or her creativity, energy, and talent, getting more and more buried under unmet obligations, unfinished projects, and piles of books or papers waiting to be read.

Whether you call this ADD, F-state, attention deficit trait, or just modern life, this way of being in the world has become common. The goal should be to turn all this into an advantage. I set the same standard in managing F-state that I do for my patients who have actual ADD: Turn it to work for you, not against you.

I tell my patients who have ADD that ADD is a gift, but a gift that is difficult to unwrap. I would say the same about modern life. It is a gift, an extraordinary gift no generation has ever seen until now. But this extraordinary gift can seem *impossible* to unwrap. Learning how to preserve C-state and, if you lose it, to get from F-state to C-state can help. (See part 2 for more tips on unwrapping.)

21 Juggling

The overloaded brain and the overloaded life have become the norm. A person has to be quite deliberate to avoid overload.

As it could for me years ago, the modern grill can get too full.

Are you too overworked to focus on your job?
Yes, I'm overwhelmed   62.8%
Only sometimes   23.0%
No, I focus fine   14.2%

—Internet poll on Boston.com, spring of 2005

New York, NY—March 15, 2005—A new study released today by Families and Work Institute, *Overwork in America: When the Way We Work Becomes Too Much,* reports that one in three American employees are chronically overworked, while 54 percent have felt overwhelmed at some time in the past month by how much work they had to complete. The study of more than 1,000 wage and salaried employees identifies for the first time why being overworked and feeling overwhelmed have become so pervasive in the American workplace.

"Ironically, the very same skills that are essential to survival and success in this fast-paced global economy, such as multi-tasking, have also become the triggers for feeling overworked," reports Ellen Galinsky, president of Families and Work Institute and a lead author of the study. "Being interrupted frequently during work time and working during non-work times, such as while on vacation, are also contributing factors for feeling overworked."

And from the *Evening Standard* in London, January 6, 2005:

Research today reveals that for most British working women, "information overload" is a major cause of stress. More than half—59 per cent—say being swamped by unnecessary information, including text messages, voicemail and emails, hampers their ability to run their lives as they wish. More than 1,000 women aged 18 and above were questioned about their work and leisure habits. Two thirds—67 per cent—claim they find it hard to "switch off" and relax. And 69 per cent have made a resolution to remedy the situation in 2005—marking a trend toward what experts are calling "life simplification." Consumer planning manager Mimi Fakhri said: "Life simplification will become increasingly important in the years ahead." Tips given for a simpler life included turning off your mobile phone at specific times and prioritizing your friends with fewer but firmer plans. Women are advised not to struggle into work when ill but to stay at home and rest.

Women are advised not to struggle into work when ill but to stay at home and rest. What an image, as if out of Dickens. Imagine women all over England, feverish, aching, mentally impaired, dragging themselves in to work for fear of losing their jobs or just because they feel an obligation to do so. And look at the phrasing: "Women are advised . . ." Advised by whom? Perhaps no authority dares attach his name to such subversive advice, as if the economy and the future of England depended upon a full labor force, which now must include the sickly, the infirm, perhaps even the insane. As the title of a recent book warns us, there are now "Three Billion New Capitalists." Welcome, India; welcome, China.

As demands mount, people lose the ability to stop and think, to prioritize and to say no. Fear clouds their judgment. When such fear combines with the daily gush of information and obligations, a person's mind heats up. It can overheat and melt down. The meltdown is F-state.

I once interviewed a professional juggler. He told me the greatest number of balls he could juggle was six. The greatest anyone had ever juggled, as far as he knew, was eleven. And the most objects of any kind—rings, because they take up the least space when thrown vertically into the air—was thirteen. I asked him if he was working to get to seven balls. He told me he was not because in order to get to seven he would have to give up several hours a day for at least six months, and he didn't have the spare time to do that. "I'm very good," he told me. "I put on a great show with six. No one has ever come up to me and told me they wish I had done seven. I can work many variations with six and make people's jaws drop. Six is enough. I don't need any more." It reminded me of the limit I learned while tending the grill.

How many balls do you juggle? How many items can you put on your grill? Competition in all fields is getting stiffer as the world becomes increasingly flat. People try to juggle seven balls these days to stay ahead of the pack, but often they don't need to. They just feel they do. They feel both a fearful pressure to get busier and an irresistible urge to do so. They steal time from sleep or leisure to practice their juggling. That leaves them— us—with less sleep and less leisure. How much less can we put up with? Books like *The Progress Paradox: How Life Gets Better While People Feel Worse* by Gregg Easterbrook document that we are already less happy than our affluence would predict we should be. We don't stop to ask why, to take note, as the juggler did, that six balls is plenty to put on a good show.

Keep as many balls in the air as you can, and don't drop any. That's the modern challenge. If you're juggling more than you're comfortable with—who isn't?—do whatever you must to keep the balls in the air. If a ball drops, laugh, cry, curse, take a pill, but whatever you do, be sure to pick it up and keep juggling. Don't cut back on your balls. Enjoy the rewards of the busy life. Life has never been this good.

But it is difficult to keep picking up the balls and tossing them back into the air. Juggling is hard work. And it's not as worthwhile as thinking, feeling, or taking a shower.

22 "Folks Ain't Got No Time"

I was standing in line at Logan Airport waiting to pass through security one day when out of nowhere a man barreled into the line, waving his ticket, shouting, "I'm gonna miss my plane! You gotta let me through." His briefcase and suit couldn't conceal the primitive person he'd become as he pushed and shoved at all of us. Lurching ahead, he knocked an elderly man to the floor and didn't even notice he'd done it.

As I helped the old man to his feet, he put his arm on my shoulder and said, "Thank you, thank you."

"Are you all right?" I asked.

"I'm just fine, my friend, just fine. I'm always glad to be alive. But that man there, he's got problems. Folks just ain't got no time no more."

I smiled at my new friend and said, "Ain't *that* the truth." He smiled back at me, and we spent the rest of our time in line talking to each other about life and the Boston Red Sox.

Writing this book, I often think of that friend, whom I never saw again. Since, as my friend said, nobody got no time, who's gonna read what I write? Why write if no one reads? But then I think, maybe people will at least have time to take a bite out of it.

Not having time to read the book, people might make time to eat it. We often eat books these days, just as we eat magazines and newspapers and any other written material bearing more words than a billboard.

We used to read books all the way through, at least now and then. No time for that now. Now we want the abstract, the gist, the elevator pitch, the dumbed-down version, the bare bones, the meat, just the facts, the CliffsNotes, the Classics Illustrated version. At Harvard Business School, students are taught how to 80/20 an article, business plan, or other piece of writing. To 80/20 a piece, you flip through it, mentally excising the 20 percent that will give you all you really need. (If this can be done, you have to wonder why the other 80 percent was written at all.) But even 80/20'ing can take too much time.

So we clever, modern people have devised a new way of getting at words, a method I call "eating." Eating words means doing whatever you have to do to chomp down the essentials in a written piece. You bite into this paragraph, flip a chunk of pages ahead, graze down another page or two, chew on the jacket notes, consume the table of contents, wolf down a few more paragraphs if your interest has been piqued, then close the book, most likely forever. You've eaten it. You've ripped it open and forced down all you could as time hovered over you, impatient to rush you off to some other place where you will feel rushed to go off to yet another spot. Sequential, word-by-word, page-by-page reading is *so slow*, so twentieth century. There is no time for that in this century. Somewhere else always wants us. It is waiting, foot tapping, watch watching, until we arrive. We can never fully arrive anywhere because somewhere else will pull at us once we get there. Who possibly has time to read, word by word?

It may be only a matter of time before pictures replace words altogether. And this may not be bad at all. In a brilliant book, *Thinking Like Einstein: Returning to Our Visual Roots with the Emerging Revolution in Computer Information Visualization*, Thomas West writes:

> Each technology has its limits. Long ago, Socrates described some second thoughts he had about the new and questionable technology called a "book." He thought it had several weaknesses. A book could not adjust what it was saying, as a living person would, to what would be appropriate for certain listeners or specific times or places. In addition, a book could not be interactive, as in a conversation or dialogue between persons. And finally, according to Socrates, in a book the written words "seem to talk to you as if they were intelligent, but if you ask them anything about what they say, from a desire to be instructed, they go on telling you just the same thing forever." After more than two millennia, it now seems that a new kind of technology, with interactive multimedia capabilities, may be beginning to address some of Socrates' concerns.

Books are linear. Modern life is not. Books lack pictures. The modern learning style is visual. Books contain sequences of words offered one after the other, in a prescribed order. But modern life is hunt-and-peck. Books present a coherent picture. Modern life sprays itself at you and defies you to make the picture cohere. Books can be opened to page 132, and time after time page 132 will be the same. Modern life reshuffles the pages each day and adds some new ones to boot. Modern life is neither linear nor circular. Its patterns are so difficult to decipher that it is causing more and more intelligent people to resort to simplistic, absolute conclusions just to feel the comfort of being certain, no matter if the certainty is a mirage.

This is neither good nor bad. It just is. I neither deplore it nor applaud it. But I do take note of it.

For example, if you have read this far, you are rare. An unusual event is unfolding. You have let yourself slow down enough to get more than the sound bite of this book. The sound bite is in the title. If you have read this far, you are hoping for more and you are sacrificing time you could be using to do something else to try to get that more. You can tolerate some degree of complexity. You have lingered long enough now to begin to think and feel as you read. These words are sparking ideas and feelings of your own in your imagination; you are creating your own version of this book as you read. You are making it into your own book, relating it creatively to your life or to life in general.

You have decided not to eat the book but to read it, at least for now. But you must pay for doing this. You pay with your attention. The idiom *to pay attention* has never been more apt, because the cost of attention has never been this high. The cost is all that you must deny your attention—a dizzying list of other readily available targets—by placing it here. It is more and more difficult for most of us to focus on any one target for long because our collective attention has been trained of late to surf, to be poised to dart off the moment it arrives, like a hummingbird at a feeder.

Always valuable, your attention has now also become one of your most insecure assets and most-sought-after possessions. Advertisers spend millions to learn what captures it, yet we often give it away without meaning to as clever people and smart devices have learned how to steal it. I would love to steal it for the rest of this book, but by calling attention to your attention, I have forfeited any chance I had to steal it. I have put you in a position to consciously decide. This gives you a rare moment. Most of the time we pay attention for reasons other than that we decided to. We are seduced, tantalized, subliminally redirected, unintentionally engaged by some extraneous stimulus, or focused on some task because we are compelled to be.

But now, in this moment, you can decide—indeed, you must decide. I have given the decision over to you completely. How much longer will you keep your attention here? It is a decision you make—intentionally or unintentionally, consciously or unconsciously, advertently or inadvertently—thousands of times every day. It is the most important decision a person makes that often, yet it is most often left to chance or the direction the wind is blowing. It is especially important to think about that decision these days, as attention theft runs rampant. Only by deliberately deciding what to attend to can you protect yourself against having your attention stolen.

You must train yourself to stay on task as much as the world is training you to go off task. Attention is like money: If we don't watch how we spend it, we waste it. (For more on training your attention, see part 2.)

Think for a moment about how much time you give away without meaning to . . . to the television or radio commercial you are putting up with until you get back to the show; to the "friend" you don't really like; to the e-mail you don't need to read; to the shopping you don't need to do; to the memory of the bad thing that was done to you years ago; to the hundredth time you've worried about the same matter that's out of your control; to the nails you can't stop biting.

The more you give it away, the less you have left for what

you need. Attention isn't infinite, nor is the energy required to focus it.

So to give your attention to this page and to this book, you ought to get something of value back—or you ought to close the book. In exchange for your attention I offer you information, insight, and entertainment pertaining to the crazy life so many of us (myself included) live these days. Is that worth your time?

If you are here now, you're not somewhere else, which is what makes it difficult at any time to be here now. The injunction "Be here now," which on the face of it sounds impossible *not* to do, is in fact difficult because of the many magnets pulling attention anywhere *but* here.

Furthermore, it's not an easy question, where are you now. I didn't put a question mark at the end of that sentence because it was a statement, not a question. I add that comment just in case the lack of a question mark distracted you, but also to point out how small a stimulus it takes to distract us, the lack of a question mark, how small a force can take a person away from being here, on this page—or anywhere, for that matter.

Are you still with me?

You want to find out *now* what the value added will be of reading this, to use business-speak. If I don't convince you right off the bat to stay with me, you won't. I want you to stay because I have a sense of what you're up against in your daily life; almost all of us are up against the same thing. This book is about that thing—and how to deal with it.

It's about how much you have on your mind. It's about how little can steal you away. Major issues take your attention, but so do many minor issues—such as, maybe you're thinking "right off the bat" was a cliché. It is, but I like to write in an informal style that makes room for clichés. I could have said, say, "right off the hockey stick," but that would have distracted you, even as this discussion is probably making you impatient. You want me to make my point, to spit it out.

These days a person has to both get to the point fast and keep the point simple, no matter how complex it is. The problem is that life has never been more complex.

I hope you're still here. Why should I care? What do I want with you? Yup, that's another question modern life makes us ask faster than ever before. Since we have so little time to give, and so many people want what little we have, we ask, right off the bat, What does *he* want? We are so accustomed to smooth tongues sashaying into predictable pitches that we are poised to hang up the phone—or change the station, or walk away, or flip the page, or close the book—the very second we detect an agenda that puts us off or that we've heard before.

What it takes to please now is trickier than ever because the competition is so clever. Furthermore, what's pleasing may be simplistic. Indeed, life is so complex that we get tired of wrestling with it and we crave something simple. That's why politicians and CEOs use simple slogans; the masses rally around them. And don't be deceived: We're *all* part of the masses.

To hold your attention, shall I buffet you with arresting bullet points? (Even the term *bullet point* reflects what we're up against. Bits of data should be like bullets in order to penetrate.) Okay. Which of these is true?

- The population of the world will triple in the next three years.
- Global warming will transform the climate of Boston into the climate of Brazil by 2009.

- By 2010, we will wear computers the size of wristwatches powered by the surface electricity of our skin with screens provided through retinal implants.
- By 2011, we will not need to read to learn but instead have information implanted directly into our brains through the development of nanotechnology.

As far as I know, only the third item is not too much of a stretch. The other events may well transpire, unless things change. I may just have the dates wrong. But that's not my point. My point is that even arresting facts may not arrest us because we have grown so accustomed to reading or hearing them. What was once the banality of evil has become the banality of everything. So much is arresting that nothing is.

Everybody harvests the Internet and comes back with more arresting facts than the *National Enquirer*. None of us has time to check out these facts, so we take them in, feeling a passing sense of shock dulled by skepticism, and then we let the arresting facts drift into the bloated brain file called "Stunning Information That I Will Soon Forget."

What is the sound bite of this book? I should have put it in the title or made it clear many pages ago or I would have lost you long before now.

That's the point. Instead of thoughtful lives they savor, people are in danger of living superficial, sound-bite lives they barely notice, let alone savor.

I'll put it differently. Something alarming is happening to this world, which I'm discussing with you in this book. Keeping in mind that the smartest people on earth once thought the world was flat, and keeping in mind that the most brilliant people alive once had no idea that our planet was spinning a mile a minute (actually faster than that) on its axis, circling the sun, and tilting back and forth, we might well wonder what fundamental assumptions we have all wrong today. It may be that we're going too fast now to operate by the old methods any longer. But which of the old methods are we going to discard, and where are the new ones we will replace them with? If we're not careful, we'll discard what we need most. By doing what we imagine the smartest people are doing, we may be doing it all wrong.

We might imagine the smartest people are *fast*. Fast is with-it, slow is dull, or so we might believe. Then we start to get rid of what matters most.

For instance, we may get rid of love and thought. If we're not careful, the acts of feeling and thinking deeply will increasingly become an activity of the few. Being stimulated or providing stimulation will become the activity of the many. The content won't matter as long as it is catchy—that is, stimulating.

Gradually, imperceptibly (if we're not careful), we will feel closer to Katie Couric (who I think is great) or the cast of *Everybody Loves Raymond* and *Law & Order* (both of which I watch and enjoy) than to our friends and neighbors—and we'll certainly see them more often. We will be stimulated electronically for many hours every day, taking in millions of bits of stuff we will quickly forget, stupid stuff that held our precious, irreplaceable attention for a few moments via TV, cell phones, e-mails, video games, computer screens, the Internet, and the like. This glittering, rhinestone stream of stimulating irrelevance will pass through our consciousness so quickly that it will have no time to grow into a thought or idea of our own. It will simply set off a feckless series of synaptic events that amount to nothing that lasts long.

People opt for this because thinking and feeling deeply take way too much time and effort. It is more convenient to have thoughts and feelings packaged for us by commentators. Life increasingly becomes an instant replay: Reflexively, we don't know what to think of what we saw until someone slows it down, replays it, and tells us what it was really all about. Tell me what to invest in, whom to vote for, what to eat, what to watch, how to live, and ultimately what to feel and think. More and more, people want their thoughts packaged and given to them—Abortion is murder! Abortion is a woman's right!—so that they can then use them merely for a source of stimulation as they beat one another over the head with received ideas.

Don't you think you could write the average right-wing book or left-wing book yourself? People who read them (and I have read a few) do so not to learn anything new, but to get worked up about what they already "think," thoughts that were previously given to them.

People do this not because they are stupid, but because they go so fast and take on so much that they don't have time to do what is most rewarding and useful—namely, to think and feel for themselves. They revert to what is training them: rapid-fire stimulation.

Ideas should be served up next to the rotisserie chickens at the fine foods market where we stop on the way home from work—work, where we have been commanded to think as little as possible while "producing" as much as we can.

The efficient worker, like the efficient parent, the efficient homemaker, or even the efficient lover, does much better not to think or feel in depth. That simply slows things down. While thoughts and emotions themselves come fast, putting them together into a coherent whole takes time. It can even hurt, giving

you a headache. It is so much easier to have someone else—
someone smarter, someone more experienced—do it for you.
Even pro quarterbacks don't call their own plays anymore. How
can any of us presume to call ours?

But, of course, we want to call our plays. And, of course, we
should. To do that, though, we have to protect our attention and
time. If you juggle too much, you'll eat books.

23 Speed's Appeal

Got it. Next point.

Don't you just *hate* to wait?

Today people get the picture quickly—or think they do. As Malcolm Gladwell points out in his book *Blink: The Power of Thinking Without Thinking,* we are wired with the ability to recognize patterns before we analyze them consciously. "Long-winded" might be defined as the tendency to insist on analyzing the patterns after we have recognized them. But "impulsive" might be defined as the tendency never to look past first impressions.

How long do you need before you decide if you like someone? Who or what gets a second look? In this busy age, a new person or idea is lucky to get even a first look.

We go fast not just because we're busy, but because speed is fun. Speed grips attention. Speed excites. Speed speeds you out of boredom. *Nothing* is boring if it's fast enough.

Slow is boring. Slow is slippery. Slow is a synonym for stupid. Slow loses your attention.

Speed is the blessing (and the curse) of the modern age. It is our drug of choice, while slowness has become like poison.

Sh   than long ones. Long
senten   rds and more than one
depen   e focus and memory to
get fro   g a word or being confused   n the risk of losing the
mode   electronic communications t   :r than words, or if words
must   :es or, even better, mere
sente   )tions or labels. Are you
still v

I   )ter fast. Will you stay if I
agre

                          tion of Just About Every-
thing, james O.....   speeded up we have be
come. As he says, just about everything we do we do faster than
we used to.

I wonder why. What's our hurry? Why, as the novelist Milan
Kundera points out, is speed our new form of ecstasy? In fact,
both speed and ecstasy are slang terms for drugs of abuse, drugs
that can make you high. But even without taking a drug, modern culture associates going faster with being happier as well as
smarter.

Neither makes sense. There is no correlation between a fast
life and a happy life. Indeed, if anything there is a negative correlation, as fast lives tend to be stressful.

The common association of fast with smart (and slow with
stupid) is particularly misleading. Some people have brains that
process information quickly, while others process information
slowly. This can be measured by neuropsychological testing,
which divides people into two groups: fast processors and slow
processors. The fast processors, like Robin Williams, often daz-
zle us with their verbal dexterity, leading us to believe they are

brilliant. The slow processors, like Eeyore, keep us drumming our fingers, waiting for them to get to the point, leading us to believe they are stupid.

Nothing could be further from the truth. While the fast processor is glib and entertaining, like a stand-up comic, he is not necessarily deep or original. The slow processor, looking at everything from many angles, considering every nuance, and perceiving parts of problems not seen before, is often the more profound thinker and the more original. For example, do you know who said the following words? "Please explain the problem to me slowly, as I do not understand things quickly." It was Albert Einstein.

In this fast world, the slow processors can get easily dismissed, overlooked, or devalued. They are some of our wisest, most talented minds, and we would do well to wait while they think and to stop and listen when they speak, even if they do so slowly.

We love speed not because it is deep, original, valuable, or important. We love it mainly because it is exciting. Going fast to the point of inducing fear causes an adrenaline rush. This is the adrenaline high. Adrenaline is, in fact, similar in its chemical structure to amphetamine, which is the drug called speed.

But the appeal extends beyond the rush you get from adrenaline. Speed becomes a matter of ego and pride. People crave speed even without an adrenaline high. When you do a jackrabbit start the second the light turns green, you don't get an adrenaline high, but you do obey a ubiquitous command: Be first. Never wait. It is one of the rules of the road that almost no one violates. Cars hurtling down highways at speeds of over 100 mph are not uncommon sights. But a car traveling at any speed less than the speed limit is rare.

When I drive to my office each morning, I have to merge onto a busy highway, Route 2 heading west from Arlington, where I live, to Sudbury, where I work. As I merge, I look into my rearview mirror to make sure I have some space to ease from the entrance ramp onto the highway. Invariably, obeying a law of nature as predictable as tides, if a car is approaching me, the car does not slow down to let me merge but instead *speeds up*, intent on denying me entry in front of him. The driver has absolutely no reason to do this other than the ego boost he gets from being in front of me rather than behind.

By being faster, he believes he is better and believes it with such fervency that he is willing to risk his life—as well as my life and the lives of the people in the cars around us—by forcing himself in front of me. In a game of chicken played on American highways tens of millions of times every day, if I don't slow down, we collide. Our love of speed—and being in front—becomes a matter of life and death.

On the other hand, we so hate to wait that we risk our lives to avoid it. Waiting is painful. Slow hurts. The quicker you get out of the starting blocks at the intersection, the quicker you can get to the next light, the quicker you can get to where you are going. But you do not reason at the light; you simply step on the gas and leave the past behind. Fast is a reflex. The DOOR CLOSE button on elevators gets pushed all the time, even when a passenger is not in a hurry. He hates to wait. No matter that he's not going anywhere. Waiting is toxic to his soul.

Of course, there are times when speed saves lives, as in an ambulance. The speed with which we can transmit information has changed the world and allowed for much of our recent progress, assuming we want to call the changes we've seen progress.

Doing a job quickly is sometimes essential, as in performing a cesarean section or in doing CPR. But most of the time, the tortoise beats the hare. Slow but sure is underrated. Fast is overrated. The news services compete to out-scoop one another, to get the news first. But what difference does it make? That's a question rarely asked.

Time limits on tests and exams force students to go as fast as they can. Students who get anxious under time limits are penalized unfairly. What difference does it make how fast you can produce the right answer, as long as you can produce the right answer? Unless you are preparing for a career on *Jeopardy!* does it really matter? Timed testing is just another example of the bias in our world that favors speed.

When the great cognitive psychologist Jean Piaget toured America, giving lectures on the stages of cognitive development he had discovered in children, he was asked one question so often that he called it "the American question." People would ask, "Dr. Piaget, we are impressed with your explanation of these stages. But could you tell us, please, how we can make our children go through them faster?"

Sometimes, forcing a process to go faster than it is meant to go does damage. Forcing children to grow up too fast is a common example. Other examples: forcing wine to age faster, forcing trees to grow faster, hurrying a golf swing, forcing love to come sooner, forcing tomorrow to come today.

As a country, we love to go fast and win the race. The problem is, we lose the great victory to be won in slowing down.

24 Where Do New Ideas Come From?

Before you read further, please stop and answer the following question: Where do you do your best thinking?

Try asking the next ten people you meet where they do their best thinking. You'll be surprised how many say, "In the shower." Or the runner-up: "In my car." Few, if any, will say they do their best thinking at work, where, it might be supposed, thinking is the order of the day.

What's so special about the shower? Furthermore, what's so special about thinking? Don't we do it automatically, all the time? And why does the workplace not produce better thinking?

To take those questions in reverse order: What a person does at work is too goal directed and contaminated by gemmelsmerch to allow the free play of ideas that great thinking requires. Work devotes itself (usually) to the rush and the gush and teems with worry, blather, and clutter.

Thinking, although sometimes overrated, is special for many reasons, chief among them: Only by thinking well will we save ourselves from destruction; only by thinking well will we discover and learn how to make use of the new ideas that advance civilization; and only by thinking well will we figure out the best way to get from here to there.

While our brains are always active, even when we are asleep, thinking is neither automatic nor constant. A moment of thinking varies in intensity and duration as much as attention does. Indeed, the two go hand in hand. Thinking, which might be defined as focused attention combined with active trapping and sculpting of the objects of focus, ranges in quality from imitative and predictable to original, from feeble to strong, from inhibited to bold. A challenge people have always faced is how to improve the quality of their thinking. Now, because of the peculiar obstacles to thought posed by modern life, that challenge is particularly formidable. One of the best ways to improve the quality, intensity, and duration of thinking is to make use of the principles outlined in this chapter.

Finally, showers promote good thinking because showers induce a state of comfort, calm, and relaxation. They stimulate all five senses: the feel of the water on the skin and the feel of the steam; the sounds of the shower; the smells of the soaps, shampoos, and whatever else is in the environs; the taste of the water; and the sight of the parts of your body that you see as you wash them, as well as the stall or the tub that you're in. This runs counter to the notion that we do our best mental work in an area free of much sensory stimulation, such as a quiet, well-lit room or a library. If not in the shower, other people say they do their best thinking while driving, which is also a place of multisensory stimulation.

Showers and the car share one more quality: When you are in them, your mind is free to go where it wants. No one is telling you what to do, what to work on, or what to think about, which gives you access to what your mind has been thinking about without your knowing it, or what is sometimes called "the unconscious." What your mind is thinking about without your knowing it is the source of your best ideas. The unconscious is like a great incubator.

You can see such incubation in the writing of a novel, or the designing of a building, or the creation of an ad campaign, or the putting together of a game plan for football, or in any effort we call creative. When at last the product is ready to venture into the world, the original idea is usually as invisible as the human egg is to a newborn baby. It has been incorporated, divided, and, most of all, developed.

The process of finding ideas and growing them, as painful and frustrating as it is, as rarely completed as it is, as demoralizing and depressing as it can be, is still the most advanced activity the human mind can engage in. It is also something the human mind can do and machines can't, at least as of yet.

Perhaps the greatest damage done by F-state is that it stifles this process, as if blocking the mind's tubes. If a person is too busy, too distracted, and too overwhelmed by data and demands, attention is not available to fertilize the egg when the germ of a new idea takes shape.

In F-state, all a person thinks about—even in the shower or while driving—is how to make the deadline, return the calls, gather the information, or reach the destinations before time runs out. This person's attention has no time for anything else. As is always the case when toxic emotions bubble up, attention loses the flexibility required for high-quality thought. Single-minded, rigid, black-and-white, low-grade thinking ensues.

The greatest danger of being overwhelmed is not that you will fail to meet your goals, but that you will fail to think at your best and to give birth to your best ideas. As was once said, the problem is not that people aim too high and miss, it's that they aim too low and hit. In F-state, you won't do what you had not expected to do. You won't notice what you weren't looking for; you won't see what wasn't there before; you won't see what had been there all along but had not been noticed; and you won't see what could be there if you were to create it.

Let me give an example of high-quality thinking from the mind of a master of new ideas, a child. In this case it is my own child, Jack, but it could be any child, as children beget more new ideas than any other group of people. They constitute our best, most unused think tank.

When Jack was eight years old, we took a trip down to Virginia and we stopped at a motel on the New Jersey Turnpike on the way. We got there around midnight, so we took just one room, figuring we could pile four of us into two queen beds and get a cot for the fifth. We undressed quickly, leaving our clothes all over the room, and promptly went to sleep.

The next morning I felt someone shaking my shoulder. Half asleep, I peered up to see who was shaking me. It was Jack. "Dad, I'm awake," he said.

"I can see that, Jack," I replied, looking over at the red digits on the clock next to the bed.

"Is it okay if I turn on the TV?" Jack asked.

"No, it's not okay," I replied. "It's six a.m. We all want to sleep. Why don't you go back to sleep, too?" With that, I turned over, pulled the covers up under my chin, and instantly fell back asleep.

Sometime later, I felt someone shaking my shoulder again. I looked up and there was Jack again. I glanced at the clock: 7:30. "Okay," I said, rubbing my eyes, "I guess it's time to get rolling."

"Dad," Jack interjected, "look what I made."

That sentence gave me pause. What had he done? Jack pointed toward the center of the room. I looked but saw only air at first. Then I looked more closely and saw a cord of some sort stretching from the handle of the window clear across the room to the doorknob on the door to our room. "What's that?" I asked.

"It's a clothesline," Jack proclaimed proudly. Staring at the cord, I could see that in fact it was a line made of clothes, all the clothes that we had left strewn about the room. Jack had picked them up, tied them together, and created his clothesline.

"Very interesting, Jack," I said. He looked up at me with a proud grin, knowing I enjoyed what he had done, also knowing that we needed to get to work untying the clothes before Mom and Lucy began looking for their clothes.

What happened in Jack's mind between 6:00 and 7:30 in that room is the force that has advanced civilization. It is at the heart of what we call creativity. I can imagine a caveman or -woman one morning feeling bored, as Jack did, scratching around on the ground, doing nothing purposefully, rolling some rocks on the ground, and gradually coming up with the idea of a wheel. Of course, what Jack invented did not change civilization, but the process of mind he engaged in was the same as the process that does.

He recombined the elements of his experience into a new form. That is what creativity is all about. Where did the idea come from to pick up the clothes and tie them together, making a clothesline? Did he think of the play on words first, *clothes* and *line*, and then make it in imitation of that? Or did he pick up one article of clothing, then another, and then absently tie them together? Did he start with the helpful idea of cleaning up the room, then get distracted by the new idea of fashioning the line?

I asked Jack about this. I asked him, "Where did you get the idea for the clothesline?"

His answer was the honest answer most people give when asked where their new ideas come from. "I don't know," he said. I pressed him, but he still did not know.

The egg of the idea rolled out from the unconscious, and Jack was relaxed enough to pay attention to it. He took it and grew it and made it into something new.

Had he been in F-state—which Jack rarely is—he would not have picked up on the idea. Of course, that wouldn't have mattered. Jack's clothesline was not an idea the world needed to have.

But the world does need to foster and protect the conditions under which he came up with the idea. If we are too busy, too overwhelmed, too goal directed and data driven, we will not notice the new ideas that roll into consciousness, and they will disappear.

To come up with their best ideas, people need time not only to stop and think, but also to fiddle around, to play with what they've got, as Jack did with the clothes on the floor. If you keep looking for more data—more clothes—you will never synthesize what you do have into something important. And if you feel excessive pressure to come up with a specific result, to reach a specific goal, you will never reach a goal you had never thought of. You will never surprise yourself or the world.

For example, the man who discovered the DNA fingerprint, a discovery that revolutionized forensic science, did so by accident. Alec Jeffreys, a professor of genetics at the University of Leicester in England, was working on an unrelated project in genetics one Monday morning when, "at 9:05"—he remembers the precise moment—he saw in a map of a strand of DNA what he had neither expected to see nor set out to find. "Suddenly I could see the potential for individual identification," said Jeffreys. "It was a question of the penny dropping very quickly. By ten o'clock, we were frantically running around the lab thinking of all sorts of possible applications."

Jeffreys hadn't set out to find any such thing, but when it appeared he was ready to see what he saw. Similarly, in 1928 when Alexander Fleming returned from a two-week vacation to see that a culture plate he had left in his lab was overrun by staphylococci except for one small spot, he did not ignore the one small spot, as some would have done. He had not expected to see what he saw, but, as he famously remarked, "Chance favors the prepared mind." His mind was prepared not only by the years of schooling he had undertaken, but also by the conditions of his mind on that September day in 1928. He was not so hurried to get organized and back into work, nor was he so distracted by thoughts of his vacation, that he could ignore the unexpected.

Furthermore, he lingered over and played with what he saw long enough to make something important of it. In fact, John Tyndall had discovered the antibacterial properties of *Penicillium notatum* in 1875, more than fifty years earlier, but Tyndall hadn't made much of it. Fleming, on the other hand, did. After penicillin had saved millions of lives and Fleming had become one of the world's most celebrated men, he remarked modestly, "My only merit is that I did not neglect the observation and that I pursued the subject as a bacteriologist."

You will not weave your data into a DNA-fingerprinting technique, penicillin, or anything else new and important if you do not notice the value of what you have or if you constantly fret that you must have more. Jean Piaget based his original and groundbreaking findings in cognitive psychology on an *n* of . . . three! His own three children. Today, his observations would be laughed out of any academic journal he might submit them to. "Woefully insufficient data," would come the reply. But those very data changed the face of psychology forever.

Today's world provides us with too much data and not enough thought. Too many destinations we're in a rush to get to and not enough detours. Too much F-state and not enough C-state.

Coleridge's Ancient Mariner found himself becalmed in an ocean of salt water when he uttered his famous lament, "Water, water everywhere, / Nor any drop to drink." The modern equivalent of that salt water is data. We see data everywhere we look, as far as the eye—or optic cable—can see, but most people die before turning it into a liquid they can drink. The scientific method has so cowed the average thinker that she can't act on what she has; she needs more data. So she busily sets out to get it, ignoring in her hurry the nuggets by her side.

Such busy thinking, rather than bold thinking, has plagued us long before this current busy era. Think how long the world existed, all but begging to not be deemed flat, before someone proposed that it actually might not be flat. For thousands of years, humans, equipped with the same brain we have today, looked out at the horizon and shuddered at the idea of sailing off the edge of the earth into the waiting jaws of sea monsters. Before laughing condescendingly at their ignorance, we all should shudder today, because doubtless we are as wrong today as pre-1492 people were then about some belief as fundamental as the shape of the world. It will take innovators to find out what our wrong beliefs might be. Let's hope we're not too hurried to listen.

What separates the great innovator from the mere data gatherer is the ability to stop gathering data and think about what has been gathered. Alexander Fleming thought long enough about what John Tyndall had observed fifty years before to help others make penicillin out of it. To recombine elements of your experience—the data—into new forms is the act that makes the difference. The surgeon who develops a new procedure, the chemist who synthesizes a new molecule, the football coach who develops a new play—all these people stop to think and play with what they have. They do what Jack did in the motel room early one morning. They fiddle around with what they've got. They play with it.

As I have explained before, by "play" I do not mean merely what a child does at recess, although that is certainly play. But the broader meaning of play is an activity that can withstand the gemmelsmerch of modern life; it is an activity that lifts a person out of the mundane into the most meaningful and productive realm. Its essence is the engagement of the imagination. Any activity that lights up your brain, that activates your imagination, is what I mean by play. A person at play can work very hard. Consider how hard a poet works writing just one line, or how hard a basketball player works developing just one new shot, or how hard an investor works picking one new stock. All of these activities engage the imagination and require a flexibility of mind that F-state shuts down.

Once in play, however, a person is temporarily safe from F-state. The imagination creates a force field around focus that will not allow any extraneous debris to penetrate. Play (that is, imaginative engagement in any activity) is the kryptonite of gemmelsmerch.

Play lies at the heart of creativity. Play can waste great quantities of time, in that it is not programmable to produce results on cue. Play goes off on tangents, knows no timetable, and can be subversive. But when play goes right, when the planets of mind align, play transforms an old place into a new one.

\\\

Part Two

Creating a System That Works for You

25 The Central Solution

You need a system The modern forces of gemmelsmerch, the rush, the gush, screensucking, fuhgeddomania, the megaloctopus, and gigaguilt will overpower you if you do not have a plan to defeat them. If you're having no trouble, you've already created your system intuitively, on your own. But if, like so many people, you feel frantic, you need a system that's based on your own needs, obligations, and personal makeup to take charge of your life.

The central solution I offer in this book is this: *Make sure you do what matters most to you.* Everything else in this book is offered in support of that one goal. In order to reach it, you must regain the measure of control you ought to have and live actively, consciously, according to a system *you* have formulated yourself, which includes the creation of a positive emotional environment and your life's right rhythm.

This is not simple. That's why I've written a book, not a paragraph. Many factors have to be taken into account, most notably the unique obstacles of our modern age.

If you don't manage the rush, the gush, and the clutter, they will sweep you away like a toothpick in a typhoon. Modern life sweeps people away every day, crashing them onto the beach of the evening tattered, exhausted, spitting sand, and ready to collapse. According to a 2005 study from the Families and Work Institute, about one-third of employees in the United States feel overworked or overwhelmed by the amount of work they have to do. While no one has total control over his or her life, most people have more control than they exert.

If you don't have a strategy, you will almost certainly find that forces such as gemmelsmerch, the megaloctopus, gigaguilt, screensucking, leeches, doomdarts, taildogging, kudzu, pile-on, and frazzing will take over your life, stealing your time and attention, draining your mental energy, forcing *their* plan upon you, leaving you feeling helpless to do anything but struggle to keep from drowning as the tidal wave flings you forward.

Keep in mind that while the central solution asks you to take charge, it cautions against seeking complete control. As I stated in the opening of this book, the search for total control is part of the problem. I call it the "control paradox": Once you pass a certain point, the more you try to gain control, the less control you have. This is because the process of trying to gain complete control drains so much of your time, attention, and energy that you have little left with which to exert the control you worked so hard to gain.

The key is to find the right balance between control and lack of control. The Serenity Prayer, purportedly written by Reinhold Niebuhr and quoted widely in Alcoholics Anonymous, puts this idea well:

> God grant me the serenity
> to accept the things I cannot change;

courage to change the things I can;
and wisdom to know the difference.

However, in today's world I would take it one step further. It is important to accept and "let be" even some things that you could change but don't have time to, if you want to preserve the right rhythm in your life. What sets the rhythm is up to you, of course. For some it is breakneck speed. But for most of us, it is slower than the forces that surround us, tempt us, or try to push us to go.

I take the liberty here of modifying the Serenity Prayer according to my purposes in this book:

God grant me the serenity to accept the things I cannot
 change;
The insight to prioritize wisely what I want to change;
The patience to resist trying to control everything I could,
 had I the energy and time;
The courage and skill to change the things I have chosen to
 change;
And the wisdom to know the differences among all these.

Once you have agreed that if you don't take back some control, it will continue to be taken from you, leading you to become ever more busy, then the question becomes how to do it. I have already suggested some tactics, and the chapters that follow suggest more.

26 Accepting Limits: The First Step Toward Doing What Matters Most

Do you know where your time goes? Many people budget their money down to the last penny (my wife and I don't, because it makes us anxious, and it is boring, an odd combination of emotions). However, I don't know anyone who budgets his or her time down to the last minute or second. I guess some Very Important People have this done for them, but even they probably have a large daily fudge factor.

If you ask adults how much money they make a year, with a few eccentric exceptions, they can tell you. If you ask them to calculate how much they would make over the next decade or even over a lifetime, they could give you a pretty good estimate if you allowed half a minute for them to calculate. People can also give estimates of how much various other people make, and the estimates will be close.

Most people know, at least within a few thousand dollars one way or the other, not only how much they make, but how much they spend, what they spend it on, what they plan to spend it on, what they are saving for, what they have wasted money on, what their bad habits with money are, what changes they would like to make in their financial lives, and what their history with money is—and they know, or can speculate, about these facts in other people's lives.

In addition, many people read books about money, they read newspaper and magazine articles about money, they pay for advice from experts about money, and they may retain a financial counselor who is always on call. The study of money is a major academic subject for which a Nobel Prize is given every year.

But time, a far more precious asset than money, rolls on unnoticed. We spend it. We waste it. We even kill it. Killing time. It's worse than burning money. Sages through the ages have cautioned us to seize the day, to make the most of the moment, to live each day as if it were our last, but rare is the person who truly does that. Time is a finite resource, but we behave as if it were infinite because, at the deepest level, we deny the fact of death in our everyday lives.

Sometimes something happens that forces us to confront death not in the abstract but as the stark fact that it is. It may be the diagnosis of a malignant cancer. It may be a narrow escape from a potentially fatal accident. It may be the sudden, unexpected death of a friend.

In my case it was a simple question from a three-year-old girl. I was forty-two at the time and had been smoking cigarettes for more than twenty years. Then one day my daughter, Lucy, looked up at me as I sat on the stoop smoking a Parliament and asked, "Daddy, when are you going to stop sucking on cigarettes?"

In that moment I understood, in a way I never had before, that I was denying my own mortality. I was pretending that cigarettes wouldn't kill me. But when the person for whom I most needed to stay alive innocently asked me when I was going to stop doing something that could kill me, my brain shook and I saw what I had chosen not to see. I was going to die someday. How could I be so reckless and stupid as to court death and risk leaving Lucy sooner than I needed to?

I never smoked another cigarette after that. Cold turkey? It was more like cold sweats.

We ought never to forget that any day might be our last. We ought to do whatever it takes to live to the fullest while we can. Only a fool would say this doesn't matter.

Or a person who is too busy to think. Being busy is one deft way to avoid taking stock of how you are living your life, knowing death is only a heartbeat away. The busy person might say, "I'm too busy to think about that. How can I ponder death when I have three loads of laundry to do and a meeting to prepare for?"

I ask you, "How can you not?" Just as Lucy brought me up short, each person ought to bring himself or herself up short and ask, "Am I doing what I really want to do? Am I doing what matters most to me?" Don't let being busy take you away from that. If it does, then being busy is slow suicide, just like smoking cigarettes—and it's just as addictive.

Ultimately, how you decide to use your time is a reflection of who you are and what you *feel* matters most. You may think one way but feel another. For example, you may think that keeping up with your friends and making time for family dinner is most important, but you may *feel* afraid that if you don't work the extra hours, you will lose your job, and if you lose your job, all is lost. Once fear starts to govern your use of time, you cease to be true to the best of who you are, and, paradoxically, you give up your chance to live a genuine life.

Having brought up the deep issue, the fear of death, the fear of the abyss, the fear of what we can't control, the need to accept the limits we face, in the next chapter I address the practical consequence of accepting the limits—namely, how you use the time you have before you die.

27 Getting the Best Return on Your Investments of Time

Investing your time wisely requires that you prioritize what you do. If you don't, leeches in the form of disagreeable people and insignificant projects will rob you of your time.

Just as people are often amazed when they look closely at how they spend their money, you may be amazed if you look closely at how you spend your time, especially if you also rank each activity that you do in terms of how worthwhile it is. Such an examination is more than a parlor game; it is one of the most telling calculations you can make.

First, let me ask you a few questions not about your bank account but about your time account. We don't usually think in terms of how much time we have, but it is a useful number to consider. Do you know how much time you have?

How many minutes in a day?
How many minutes in a week?
How many minutes in a year?
If you live to be seventy-five, how many minutes in your life?
How many minutes do you have left?

Here are the answers:

In a day, 1,440 minutes
In a week, 10,080 minutes
In a year, 525,600 minutes
In a seventy-five-year life, 39,420,000 minutes
Roughly, you have half a million minutes per year left

Assuming you live to be seventy-five (I know, we all think we will live longer, but let's go with the short-side estimate), the following table will tell you how many minutes you have left, starting at age twenty-five, in five-year increments:

Age Now	Minutes Left Until 75 Years Old
25	26,280,000
30	23,652,000
35	21,024,000
40	18,396,000
45	15,768,000
50	13,140,000
55	10,512,000
60	7,884,000
65	5,256,000
70	2,628,000
74	525,600
74 years 11 months	43,200
74 years 11 months 30 days	1,440
74 years 11 months 30 days, 23 hours	60
74 years 11 months 30 days 23 hours 59 minutes	1

I find that "1" at the bottom alternatively unimaginable and chilling.

Of course, in the true spirit of the denial of death, you could look at that table and say, "Well, of course, I am going to live to be a hundred and have my birthday celebrated by Willard Scott on the *Today* show." Assuming that you are old enough for Willard still to have that gig, you can simply readjust the numbers in the column. Whatever you insert as the age at which you estimate you will die, the numbers in those last four rows will be the same.

You may groan and say, "Oh yeah, I already know about that, I'm supposed to seize the day and all that. Fine. I'll leave that to the philosophers and preachers." But please bear with me. This is not a sermon. It is a *compilation of facts*, much as an accountant might provide regarding your finances. You wouldn't blow him off, right? (Actually, that's what my wife and I try to do with our accountant, but he won't let us, bless his heart.)

You already know the size of your bank account, and now you have an idea of the size of your time account. As your newly appointed time accountant, let me ask you a few more questions both about how you spend your time and about how you think other people spend their time.

How many hours do you work a day?
How many hours do you think the average American (AA)
    works a day?
How many hours a day do you watch TV?
How many hours a day does the AA watch TV?
How many hours do you sleep a day?
How many hours does the AA sleep a day?

Before I give the answers, let me explain where the average American data came from. The Bureau of Labor Statistics, a division of the U.S. Labor Department, did a survey of 21,000

Americans in 2003 and updated the data in 2005. It is called the American Time-Use Survey (ATUS). The participants were over the age of fifteen. They were asked to keep track of one day, called their diary day, and report exactly what they did from 4:00 a.m. of that day to 4:00 a.m. the following day. They kept exact track of twenty-four hours. (Have you ever done that?)

The surveyors then broke down the daily activities into four broad categories: sleep, leisure, work, and household duties. Based on this survey, the average day for an average American breaks down as follows:

Sleep	8.6 hours
Leisure	5.1 hours
Work	3.7 hours
Household	1.8 hours
Variety of activities, including eating, drinking, attending school, and shopping	4.8 hours

Before you gasp at the 3.7 hours per day spent working, keep in mind that the survey included many people who were unemployed, too old to work, or in school. In fact, only 44 percent of the sample were employed. Of that 44 percent, the average number of hours spent working per day was 7.6.

Of the entire sample, 96 percent reported some leisure hours (one wonders how the other 4 percent could have no downtime). Of leisure time, 50 percent was spent watching TV, or an average of 2½ hours per day. Socializing was the next highest, coming in at 45 minutes per day.

The 8.6 hours spent sleeping is as misleading as the statistic of 3.7 hours for work, because there is a great spread in the number of hours of sleep people get. When there is a great spread, averages are deceiving. In fact, according to a 2001 National Sleep Foundation survey, two-thirds of Americans do not get the recommended eight hours of sleep per night. These people are stealing from their sleep to work more. Of those surveyed, 38 percent reported working 60 or more hours per week.

So there appears to be one group of people who are working very hard and not getting enough sleep and another group of people who are either in school, unemployed, or retired and do get enough sleep. Both groups report watching at least 2½ hours of TV a day, and both groups spend 1 to 2 hours doing housework or yardwork.

Where do you fit?

A Systematic Assessment of Use of Time and Value Received for Time Invested

How do you allocate your time? You probably have some idea, but I doubt you've actually sat down and counted the minutes — as you do so often for your bank account. In a moment, I am going to provide you with a grid — adapted, but significantly altered, from the ATUS. Using this grid, you can take an organized look, perhaps for the first time, at how you allocate your hours and how you value each activity.

Have you ever done this before? I don't know anyone who has. People in business may have to submit an accounting of their time, but they do not rate the value of that time, as this form asks you to do. It is foolish indeed that we so commonly make detailed accountings of our money but almost never do so of our time and energy.

Before providing the grid, let me introduce you to it. I included various categories that the ATUS did not include, such as electronic time (separate from television), intimate time (cuddling, lovemaking, and intimate conversations, separate from the socializing category), wasted or forgotten time, and creative time. By creative time, I mean time spent thinking, daydreaming usefully, conversing creatively with a colleague, and the like. Both wasted time and creative time may often occur while doing something else, such as housework or watching TV. Enter "Creative Time" and "Wasted Time" as independent elements, so that your total number of hours can exceed twenty-four per day. I also broke down many of the elements into separate parts, such as time spent doing work you like and time spent doing work you don't like, socializing with people you like and socializing with people you don't like.

After the hours spent on each activity, I included a rating of the effort required to perform each activity. Of course, the effort will vary during the activity, and it will also vary from day to day. When you rate it, just put down what it averages out to be from your experience. Be careful not to rate it as you wish it were but as it actually has been, on average. On this scale, you can rate your effort from 5 (little effort required) to 1 (maximum effort required). Note that this rating is in reverse of the others, 5 to 1 rather than 1 to 5: The highest expenditure of effort gets the lowest rating number, and the lowest expenditure gets the highest rating number.

The reason for the reverse order is that later, when you calculate what I call the "worth-it factor," you must multiply effort times fulfillment times another factor called the "necessity/right-thing-to-do factor." Effort is the only one of these three factors that makes an activity potentially less worth-it the larger it gets. Therefore, the effort rating scale uses the highest number, 5, to indicate the lowest amount of effort and the lowest number, 1, to indicate the greatest amount of effort. If this is confusing, please bear with me. The arithmetic is simple, and the numbers you get will be meaningful.

Third, I included a rating I call the "fulfillment factor." Some activities leave you feeling fulfilled, while others leave you feeling frustrated or depleted, regardless of how much effort they required. Use a rating from 1 to 5 here. If an activity is highly fulfilling, give it a 5. If it is utterly unfulfilling, give it a 1.

Once you have rated the effort and fulfillment factors, you can tabulate a simple product, effort times fulfillment. A maximum effort (score = 1) multiplied by minimum fulfillment (score = 1) yields a product of 1. That's the lowest score possible and indicates either that you're crazy to be doing this activity or that you are being compelled to do it by someone else, by necessity, or by your values. If this product, effort times fulfillment, is less than 5, you may not be getting enough fulfillment for your effort and you might try to make a change, if that's possible.

But the score is not definitive. For example, some of the activities most worth preserving in your life will get a score of 5. These are the activities that require maximum effort (score = 1) and yield maximum fulfillment (score = 5) for a product of 5. For me, writing a book is such an activity. Nothing in my professional life takes more work, but writing books is hugely fulfilling for me. Its effort-times-fulfillment product is 5, but it is not an activity I should cut. The score of 5 is just a red flag to take a second look at that activity and decide if it is one you want to continue.

To help assess what to do when that product is less than 5, I included the necessity/right-thing-to-do factor. This reflects your

rating of how necessary a given activity is or how much you believe you ought to do it simply because it is right or in keeping
with your beliefs. If an activity is not essential, like watching TV,
give it the lowest rating, 1. If an activity is essential, like sleep,
give it the highest rating, 5. If it is somewhere between not essential and essential, rank it 2, 3, or 4.

Similarly, if you deeply believe it is the right thing to do,
give it a 5. For example, you may not want to go visit a certain
relative whom you do not much like, but for the sake of family
togetherness you think it is the right thing to do. This visit would
take a lot of time, would require a lot of effort, would lead to
minimal fulfillment, and is not, strictly speaking, necessary.
However, you would give it a 5 because you rank it high in terms
of the right thing to do.

To return now to the effort-times-fulfillment product, the
only justification for doing an activity that produces a product
less than 5 is that it carries a high necessity or right-thing-to-do
factor. For example, paying bills requires a lot of effort and is
usually not very fulfilling. Its effort-times-fulfillment product is
less than 5. However, it is highly necessary. Therefore, this activity must go on.

On the other hand, let's say you regularly attend a financial
discussion group in order to learn how to handle money better.
It takes a lot of effort to carve out the time, and just being at the
meeting requires effort because you find it impossibly dull.
You've done it for six weeks and so far have gotten little out of it.
Its effort-times-fulfillment product is less than 5, and its necessity
factor is low. Therefore, this is an activity you probably should
discontinue.

This naturally leads to the most important number on the
grid, the worth-it factor. You multiply effort (column III) by

fulfillment (column IV) by necessity/right-thing-to-do (column VI) to get the worth-it factor. By comparing the worth-it factor to the hours spent on the activity, you will be able to see, in numbers as cold and clear as those on your bank statement, if you are spending your time wisely—*wisely having been defined by your own ratings.*

The reason that it is worth calculating the effort-times-fulfillment product as its own score before calculating the worth-it factor is that some activities may be completely unnecessary yet highly fulfilling and requiring much effort. An example might be playing the violin, if the violin is your hobby. Or composing a business plan for the great idea the entrepreneur in you is dreaming of developing. Or writing a proposal for the book you have always wanted to write. Each of these would get an effort-times-fulfillment product of 5; maximum effort (1) times maximum fulfillment (5). As each is unnecessary, the worth-it factor would be a low score, only 5. Nonetheless, each of these represents time well spent indeed.

In general, you would like your worth-it scores to be 25 or higher. For example, let's say you spend twenty minutes a day in the shower. You give it a 5 on effort (virtually no effort required), a 5 fulfillment factor (you love the shower), and a 5 necessity factor (assuming you consider being clean a necessity). This makes a worth-it factor of 125, the highest possible. Considering you spend only twenty minutes in the shower, that time is preeminently worth it. Or, to use my vocabulary, taking a shower is one of the lilies in your life.

On the other hand, let's say you spend an hour a day screen-sucking (combined unnecessary screen time). This gets an effort factor of 5 (no effort), a fulfillment factor of 1 (no fulfillment), and a necessity factor of 1 (totally unnecessary), for a worth-it factor of 5.

The only way you could get a lower worth-it factor would be if the useless activity took a lot of effort. Amazingly enough, we all do even those activities now and then. An example would be socializing with someone you do not like. The effort factor here is 1: lots of work required. Fulfillment factor is 1 (no fulfillment; if anything, negative fulfillment). The necessity factor is also 1 (totally unnecessary, unless there is some professional reason you must socialize with this person), and the right-thing-to-do factor is 1 as well, unless you believe it is "right" to spend time with people you don't like out of pity or guilt. These ratings give a worth-it factor of 1, the lowest possible score.

Activities with a rating of 1 constitute the worst leeches in your life. These drain you for no good reason. If at all possible, pull these leeches off you and out of your life.

This is not to say you have to stop watching TV or doing other seemingly unnecessary activities. For some people, watching TV is an activity that recharges their batteries and helps them relax. For such people, watching TV could get a necessity rating of 3, 4, or even 5 and a fulfillment factor equally high, which results in a high worth-it factor.

In general, any activity with a worth-it factor below 5 deserves serious consideration of being eliminated or cut back. The score is merely a red flag; look twice at this activity. Any worth-it factor totaling 25 or higher represents a good investment of your time. Those activities that fall between 5 and 25 are worth a second look. Ask yourself what you might do to make those scores higher.

The point here is to rate your activities not in terms of their absolute value—that is an undefined calculation—but in terms of their value *to you*. You alone decide. Your rating rules. How worth it is it for you to invest your time, energy, and attention in a given activity, realizing that in this busy world most people unwittingly squander these precious resources? Answering that elusive but vital question is the reason for encouraging you to do the work of filling in this elaborate grid.

Here, then, it is. I understand that it is long and that it might require an effort factor of 1 (maximum effort!) to fill in, but I am confident you will find that it will give you an unusually high worth-it factor by providing you with possibly life-changing data that you have never looked at before.

I. Activity	II. Average Hours per Day	III. Effort Factor (1 = most, 5 = least)	IV. Fulfillment Factor (1 = least, 5 = most)	V. E x F (column III x column IV)	VI. Necessity, Right-Thing-to-Do Factor (1 = least, 5 = most)	VII. Worth-It Factor (product of columns III, IV, and VI)
PERSONAL CARE (TOTAL HOURS):						
Sleep						
Eating						
Bathroom						
Shower						
HOUSEHOLD (TOTAL HOURS):						
Housework						
Food (prep and cleanup)						
Laundry						

I. Activity	II. Average Hours per Day	III. Effort Factor (1 = most, 5 = least)	IV. Fulfillment Factor (1 = least, 5 = most)	V. E x F (column III x column IV)	VI. Necessity, Right-Thing-to-Do Factor (1 = least, 5 = most)	VII. Worth-It Factor (product of columns III, IV, and VI)
Lawn and other outdoor work						
Purchasing goods and services (food, car maintenance, etc.)						
Professional services (doctor, haircutter, etc.)						
Caring for/ helping household members						
Caring for/ helping nonhousehold members						
WORK AND WORK-RELATED ACTIVITIES (TOTAL HOURS):						
The part of work you like best						
The part of work you like least						

I. Activity	II. Average Hours per Day	III. Effort Factor (1 = most, 5 = least)	IV. Fulfillment Factor (1 = least, 5 = most)	V. E x F (column III x column IV)	VI. Necessity, Right-Thing-to-Do Factor (1 = least, 5 = most)	VII. Worth-It Factor (product of columns III, IV, and VI)
The part of work that's in-between						
DRIVING, COMMUTING, TAXIING (TOTAL HOURS):						
EDUCATIONAL ACTIVITIES (TOTAL HOURS):						
ORGANIZATION, CIVIC, AND RELIGIOUS ACTIVITIES (VOLUNTEER, UNPAID) (TOTAL HOURS):						
Organizational						
Civic						
Religious						
LEISURE (TOTAL HOURS):						

I. Activity	II. Average Hours per Day	III. Effort Factor (1 = most, 5 = least)	IV. Fulfillment Factor (1 = least, 5 = most)	V. E x F (column III x column IV)	VI. Necessity, Right-Thing-to-Do Factor (1 = least, 5 = most)	VII. Worth-It Factor (product of columns III, IV, and VI)
SOCIALIZING (TOTAL HOURS):						
With people you like a lot						
With people you don't much like						
With people in between						
Playing a sport						
Other exercise						
ELECTRONIC TIME (TOTAL HOURS):						
E-mail (necessary)						

I. Activity	II. Average Hours per Day	III. Effort Factor (1 = most, 5 = least)	IV. Fulfillment Factor (1 = least, 5 = most)	V. E x F (column III x column IV)	VI. Necessity, Right-Thing-to-Do Factor (1 = least, 5 = most)	VII. Worth-It Factor (product of columns III, IV, and VI)
E-mail (screen-sucking)						
Internet (necessary)						
Internet (screen-sucking)						
Television (necessary)						
Television (screen-sucking)						
Telephone (landline)						
Cell phone						
BlackBerry, Trēo, etc. (necessary)						

I. Activity	II. Average Hours per Day	III. Effort Factor (1 = most, 5 = least)	IV. Fulfillment Factor (1 = least, 5 = most)	V. E x F (column III x column IV)	VI. Necessity, Right-Thing-to-Do Factor (1 = least, 5 = most)	VII. Worth-It Factor (product of columns III, IV, and VI)
BlackBerry, Trēo, etc. (screen-sucking)						
INTIMATE TIME (LOVEMAKING, CUDDLING, INTIMATE CONVERSATION) (TOTAL HOURS):						
WASTED, KILLED, OR FORGOTTEN TIME (TOTAL HOURS):						
CREATIVE TIME (TOTAL HOURS):						
OTHER (DESCRIBE) (TOTAL HOURS):						

Once you have filled in this grid, you have brought together in one place information that is all but hidden from most people's view. They think they know it, but they don't. You now do.

Remember, the scores are merely red flags, signals for you to take a second look. Any time you see an effort-times-fulfillment product under 5, or any time you see a worth-it factor under 5, look twice. Any time you see a worth-it factor from 5 to 25, take a second look as well. Do you really want to continue these activities as you are doing them now?

Worth-it scores above 25 indicate a sound investment of your time. Obviously, the higher you can push your worth-it scores, the better.

Armed with a systematic assessment like this of how you spend your time, you can defeat gemmelsmerch, rush, gush, the megaloctopus, and all the other monsters in the sea of modern life. You can be sure you never get too busy or too distracted to focus on what's most important. How? Just run your eyes down column IV, "Fulfillment," and make sure the corresponding number in column II, "Average Hours per Day," is as big as you can make it.

28 Ten Key Principles to Managing Modern Life

1. **Do what matters most to you.** Look at the table in the previous chapter for your own assessment of what it is that matters most to you. A person's *not doing* what matters most is the most common casualty of an excessively busy life. Don't spread yourself too thin. People often head into their day like a spray, where the megaloctopus quickly entraps them. Gemmelsmerch, the force of distraction, is so powerful today that if you don't deliberately protect time to do what matters most, it is likely you will not do it, or at best not give it the time it deserves. Focus on what you like best and on what you do best. There is not enough time to do everything you like, and there certainly is not enough time to try to get good at what you're bad at or spend time doing what you dislike (unless you must). Technology has allowed us to do so much more than we used to be able to do that it is tempting to try to do everything we've always wanted to do. This will run you ragged, whether you are a child or an adult.

    You must choose. You must prioritize. In order both to do well and to be happy, you must say, "No, thank you," to many people and activities.

Cultivate your lilies and get rid of your leeches. Give yourself permission to get rid of what hinders you, whether they're projects, people, or ideas. Yes, an idea can become a leech. Examples would be the idea that it is bad ever to get angry, or that it is bad ever to say no to a friend, or that it is bad to be different. Naming leeches for what they are takes some courage, but once you do it, and once you jettison them, you will have freed up a huge amount of time and positive mental energy.

Cultivating lilies has the same beneficial effect. Once you allow yourself to spend time with projects, people, and ideas that nourish you and help you to grow, you will look forward to each day more than you do right now.

Cultivating your lilies and getting rid of your leeches does not mean you become selfish. Indeed, one of the best lilies, for a lot of people, is the act of helping others. It feels wonderful and refuels the soul. Helping others is a lily, not a leech, unless you take it too far.

2. **Create a positive emotional environment wherever you are.** Positive emotion is not a frill. Emotion is the on/off switch for effective mental functioning. The best way to create a positive emotional environment is to work on keeping up positive relationships with people wherever you are. When you feel safe and secure in your surroundings, when you feel welcomed and appreciated, you think better, you behave better, you work better, and you are better able to help others. Failing to recognize this crucial fact is the chief reason so many people buckle under the busyness of modern life. When the emotional atmosphere is less than positive, people lose flexibility, enthusiasm, the ability to deal with ambiguity and complexity, patience, humor, and creativity. They become less intelligent than they otherwise are, as well as

less trusting. Therefore, they become less able to cooperate, plan, delegate, organize, anticipate, participate, and perform all the other functions essential to thriving in a busy environment.

3. **Find your rhythm.** When you find your rhythm, you allow much of your day to be taken care of by the automatic pilot in your brain, so that the creative, thinking part of your brain can attend to what it is uniquely qualified to attend to. You find your rhythm by combining many of the suggestions in this book: creating a positive emotional atmosphere, doing what you like and do best, prioritizing your use of time and using your morning burst wisely, getting rid of leeches, and so on. When you are in rhythm, you are in what athletes call "the zone" and the psychologist Mihaly Csikszentmihalyi calls "flow." Whatever you call it, research has proven that this state of mind elevates all that you do to its highest level.

4. **Invest your time wisely so as to get maximum return.** Try not to let time be stolen from you or let yourself fritter it away. Time, like money, gets wasted if you're not attentive to how you spend it. Today this is more important than ever, because today there are more clever thieves trying to steal your time than ever before. Let the Time Value Assessment from the previous chapter guide you in deciding what to add, what to preserve, and what to eliminate or cut back on.

5. **Don't waste time screensucking.** A modern addiction, screensucking is like smoking cigarettes: Once you're hooked, it is extremely tough to quit. Denied a screen for long, a screensucker can have a modern variant of a nicotine fit. He can start pacing, looking for a place to log on or switch on. I see people on airplanes or in church who are clearly showing

signs of screen withdrawal. They are twitching, scratching, looking around, reading something for a second, putting it down, looking at their watches, and in general feeling the pain of not being able to soothe themselves with a screen.

While screensucking doesn't carry the health risks that smoking cigarettes does, it can seriously limit a person's productivity and mental growth.

Do whatever you have to do to break the habit. While we don't have a "patch" to help people quit screensucking, we do have the combination of insight and structure that can do the trick. The insight is simply the recognition of the problem. Structure refers to any change in your behavior or environment you institute to help you quit. For example, moving your screen to a different room, or putting an alarm clock next to your screen to signal when you've gone past a certain amount of time, or programming your computer to beep every ten minutes, or training yourself to work for an extended period before you allow yourself a "screen break" all might help. Be creative and devise your own methods of breaking the screensucking habit.

In extreme cases, professional help is recommended. I have treated more than a few cases of screen addiction. I use the same treatments used for any other addiction: some combination of psychotherapy, cognitive-behavioral therapy, group therapy, meditation, physical exercise and dietary changes, a 12-step program, and sometimes medication.

6. **Identify and control the sources of gemmelsmerch** in your environment. Gemmelsmerch, the force that distracts a person from what he or she wants or ought to be doing, is as pervasive and powerful as gravity. To get you thinking along the right lines, here is an array of potential sources of

gemmelsmerch (in italics), along with possible ways to control or eliminate the gemmelsmerch:

a. *The computer glitch you could spend the next three hours fixing rather than doing the important work you'd love to postpone.*
   Do the important work first. Put an index card propped up in front of you that reads DO IT NOW. Such is the power of gemmelsmerch that if you don't know about it and know to resist it, it will sweep you away. It is like a riptide off a beautiful beach. If you are not warned of it, you may go swimming and never return.

b. *Magazines.*
   Move them, look the other way when you see them, or simply tell yourself they are off limits, as an alcoholic tells himself the bar is off limits, at least until your work is done.

c. *Mail that is waiting to be opened.*
   Set a fixed time to open your mail and stick to it. Unopened mail is so loaded with gemmelsmerch that it is best to keep it in another room.

d. *The computer screen only a chair swivel away from you.*
   Move the screen, even into another room if you have to. It is not so bad to have to get up and walk a few paces if it will save you from wasting hours of time.

e. *The telephone, cell phone, BlackBerry, or Trēo.*
   Turn them off. Limit the time you will take calls. For example, our pediatrician has a call-in hour every morning from 7:00 to 8:00. He takes calls at other times only if it is an emergency. Decide if you truly want to be available constantly. If you don't, then turn off your cell phone or other "portable electronic device."

f. *Television.*

Like all our other electronics, TV is great as long as you use it right. I am not one of the purists who deplore television. Quite the opposite. I watch it every day; it recharges my batteries and entertains me to no end. However, too much TV, like too much of anything, is bad for the brain. How much is too much is up to you to determine. As a rough guideline, I would set a one-hour-per-day limit.

g. *An open door that allows people to pop in.*

Close the door when you do not want to be interrupted. Put a sign on the door that reads WORKING. AVAILABLE AT ___ O'CLOCK.

h. *Other items on your to-do list that beckon the moment so what you are working on now becomes difficult or boring.*

Recognize this as a moment to take a break. Stand up, do a quick bit of exercise (jumping jacks work well, or squats), have a glass of water, meditate for three minutes, then go back to what you were working on. Try not to allow yourself to abandon what you were doing.

i. *Radio talk shows.*

Use these judiciously. They can be addicting. From NPR to sports radio to Rush Limbaugh, you can become so attached to a show that you lose focus on what you're doing and just listen to the show. I think the best time to enjoy these shows is while you're doing something else: washing dishes, sorting laundry, shaving, or when you're in your car. Turn them off elsewhere.

j. *A new idea that pops into your mind.*

Keep a pad next to you at all times (even when you are asleep, in case an idea hits you in the middle of the

night—believe me, you won't remember it in the morning no matter how much you think you will). Use this
pad to write down great ideas or stupid stuff you don't
want to forget (like, buy a quart of milk on the way
home) that pop into your mind while you are working.

k. *Guilt.*

Guilt, or its modern manifestation, gigaguilt, can slow
you down like a sea anchor, dragging insistently on
your mind. While it is hard to reason your way out of it,
it is best not to give in to it. One of my heroes, the
eighteenth-century essayist Samuel Johnson, struggled
with guilt for most of his life. When it hit him, it hit him
hard. He would stay in bed and ruminate at length or
write extended entries of self-laceration in his diaries.
None of this helped; indeed, it seemed to make the
guilt worse. I think the best way to deal with guilt is first
to address the reasonable part of it. If you have done
wrong, do your best to make up for it, apologize, make
amends or restitution, whatever. Next, have a talk with
yourself or, even better, someone else, regarding the unreasonable part. For example, let's say you feel guilty
that you can't spend more time with your ailing mother.
Explain to yourself—or the other person—why you
can't spend more time with her. Express how sad as well
as frustrated this makes you. Accept that you can't do
everything, that you do not have control over all life.
Then, when guilt arises, as it will, remind yourself that
you are doing what you can, that you have made some
difficult but necessary choices, and that while this
makes you sad and frustrated, it is the best you can do. If
you can see this unreasonable guilt for what it is—an at-

tempt to change the unchangeable facts of life—then it can become easier to let it go. But you must have worked on this in advance so when the guilt arises you will have a shorthand way of relegating it to where it belongs.

l. *Flirtatious or sexual fantasies.*

These make for some of life's best moments. Don't get rid of them, just try not to let them take over your whole day. If possible, when such a fantasy comes up, tell yourself you can think about that at another time, a time when you can give it your full attention.

m. *E-mail.*

See principle #5 on controlling screensucking.

n. *The conversation in the room next door.*

Take steps to soundproof your office. Sometimes a small white noise machine will do the trick (try SpeechPrivateSystems.com for a good selection).

o. *The mess in your office, home, yard, or car that needs to be cleaned up.*

Clutter is one of the major forces (along with the rush, gush, and worry) that have to be managed lest they not only distract but overwhelm you. You have to work at clutter every day, or it will win out. One of the best strategies is the acronym OHIO—only handle it once (whatever it is). File it, shelve it, hand it up, use it, respond to it, or *throw it away.*

p. *The important thing that you keep putting off doing.*

Procrastination is another bugaboo to watch out for. As stated above, try to adopt the motto "Do it now" and aggressively make yourself obey it whenever possible. The more you put something off, the larger it looms.

q. *The nagging physical symptom you can't make sense of but don't want to get evaluated by a doctor.*
A variation on the previous item, this kind of procrastination can cost you your life. It is best to get a friend to make the appointment and drive you to the doctor, if that's what it takes.

r. *Money.*
Money distracts us all. The best way not to have it intrude too much is to set up a plan that you follow all the time so that you feel what money you have is well taken care of, even if you worry you don't have enough, as most of us tend to do.

s. *Noise.*
You may not even notice it until there is silence. The "ambient noise" in modern urban life has reached a dull roar. Do whatever you can to reduce it, like closing a window or a door or trying to get the generators of the noise shut down.

t. *People who gain access to your consciousness in spite of your efforts to keep them out.*
Deal with the person rather than letting him or her haunt you. You may need to get help and suggestions from a friend to do this, but don't let a person take up space in your mind and poison it. You may want to look at my book *Dare to Forgive*, in which I explain that forgiving someone merely means letting go of anger, not condoning what was done. Chronic anger is a major and toxic distraction.

u. *Imagined dangers.*
The price we pay for having an imagination is that we dream up all kinds of dangers. These days, this is

not hard to do, as we are reminded of real dangers hourly. One way to deal with imagined dangers is to talk about them. This is a way of reality testing. If you are exaggerating the danger, this is a good way of finding out. And if you are not, then it will feel good to commiserate.

v. *Toxic worry.*

I have a simple 3-step plan for quelling excessive or toxic worry. Step 1: Talk to someone. Never worry alone. Connect. Step 2: Get the facts. Toxic worry usually derives from lack of information or wrong information. Step 3: Make a plan. Even if your plan doesn't work, you will feel more in control simply because you have a plan. Feeling in control reduces worry. And if the plan doesn't work, you can revise it.

w. *Office politics, domestic squabbles.*

Set a time and place to discuss what needs to be discussed. Once you know there is a time and place reserved to voice your concerns, they will become less distracting to you day in and day out.

x. *Beepers.*

Get rid of them if you possibly can. Have an answering service. If you must have a beeper, train people not to beep you unnecessarily.

y. ***Anything you can think of to get you out of what you're doing now.***

When this happens, catch yourself. You are being pulled away most likely because something about the task you're working on is bothering you. Maybe it's boring. Maybe it's difficult. Maybe it's confusing. Whatever the cause, don't leave, at least not yet. Instead of going off to the beckoning siren, take a brief break, go back to what you were working on, and see if you don't perceive it in a different light.

z. *The seemingly uncontrollable wanderings of your mind.*
This tendency, the essence of true attention deficit disorder, affects everyone now and then. Unfortunately, usually when you wander off you're not aware of it until you come back. If this happens more frequently now than before, that is a sign that something is amiss. Some possibilities to check out:

- Overloaded circuits. You have taken on too much and need to cut back.
- Lack of sleep.
- Lack of food.
- Dehydration. Get a drink of water.
- Boredom. Time to take a break.
- Stress. Your mind is trying to get away from a stressful environment. Do whatever you can to reduce the stress. Perhaps share your worry with another person and decide together how to reduce the stress.
- Depression. Sometimes depression begins with lack of mental focus.
- Of course, you might have true ADD. It is worth consulting with a professional, as treatment can be dramatically helpful.

7. **Delegate** what you don't like to do or are not good at if you possibly can. Your goal should be to be not independent, but rather *effectively interdependent.* You do for me and I'll do for you. This is what makes life possible. No one does it

all for himself. For children and adults alike, learning how to be effectively interdependent is a major life skill.

8. **Slow down.** The many opportunities and obligations most of us juggle have induced an almost reflexive internal impatience. We wake up impatient. Our resting state rarely rests, leaving us impatient even when we don't need to be. We tap the steering wheel while waiting at a red light even if we are early for our appointment. We clench our teeth when someone speaks slowly. We hate it when meal service isn't fast, even when the point of the meal is to spend time with other people. The cell phone comes out the minute the airplane touches down and the BlackBerry is at hand, ready to respond the moment the meeting gets dull. When we engage another person, even if we have plenty of time, we quickly start to wonder how much time we have for this person before the time for this engagement will, out of some imagined necessity, expire. The time for anything grows shorter every day as we hurry to get more done. Increasingly, we have grown unable to linger. But it is in lingering that we do our best thinking and connecting.

I read somewhere that if someone could invent a way for a personal computer to shut down quickly, instead of taking the twenty seconds or so it takes now, he would make a fortune. Apparently, that twenty seconds of waiting drives people berserk, or at least costs them enough time to make the person who might save them that time very rich.

Weren't labor-saving devices, like the personal computer, supposed to give us more free time? Well, they have saved us labor. Remember the manual typewriter, the rotary telephone, and handwritten letters? But oddly enough we have less free time, not more. According to Juliet Schor's research, the average American is working 160 more hours per year now than in 1960. That is one full additional month of forty-hour workweeks. But the forty-hour workweek itself seems a relic, a regimen for slackers. Schor published this information in 1991 in a book called *The Overworked American: The Unexpected Decline of Leisure.* The problem has only grown worse since 1991.

As global competition heats up and we fret that China and India will take all our jobs, American employers ask their people to work longer and longer hours, even as they cut back on support staff, so that quarterly numbers can still be reached, at least for now.

We are working harder and harder and longer and longer to maintain our standard of living, the highest standard of living in the world, even though we are far from the happiest people in the world. Studies that measure this sort of thing put us in the middle of the pack.

If we want to be as happy as can be, and if we want to preserve our position in the world, we will do so by thinking harder and feeling more deeply, not frantically trying to put in ever more hours.

So slow down. Stop and think. Ask yourself, "What's my hurry?" Take the question literally. What *is* your hurry? It is a lot of rushing around, trying to squeeze in more stuff than you should, thereby leading you to do all of it less well and making all of it less enjoyable. Your hurry, in other words, is your enemy. The next question is, "*Why* hurry?" Your answer probably will be, "Because I must." But that is just not true. If you go through the Time Value Assessment carefully, you will find activities you can cut out or cut back, thereby freeing up some time. Don't fill all that time with new activities, but instead let the rest of what you do proceed more leisurely. By doing this, you can slow down. This will make you both more effective and more fulfilled.

9. **Don't multitask ineffectively,** or do what I call frazzing. Give one task your full attention. You will do it better. You may eventually get so good at it that your conscious mind can attend to other aspects of the task than the menial ones. A good example of this is playing a new piece on the piano. As you practice it, you implant it in your brain, recruiting neurons from your cerebellum that make playing the piece more and more automatic. You then do not have to focus on each note as you strike it, but you can let your fingers get to the notes on their own. You—your consciousness—can focus on expression, modulation, and all the more sophisticated aspects of playing the piece. This is in fact the *only* way a human can multitask effectively—practice one action so thoroughly that it becomes automatic, thus freeing up neurons to attend to matters other than the menial aspects of the task.

10. **Play.** By my definition, this means imaginatively engaging with what you are doing. This will naturally bring to bear the best part of your mind. You will not waste time. You will improve whatever it is you are doing, and you will discover new ways of doing it or improve on old ones. You will not get distracted as easily. You will be both more efficient and more effective in whatever it is you are doing, from carrying on a conversation to making an apple pie.

To sum up the ten principles succinctly:

1. Figure out what matters most to you, then do what matters most to you. Don't get sidetracked. Cultivate your lilies and get rid of your leeches.

2. Create a positive emotional environment. This is best done by developing positive connections with people.
3. Find your rhythm. This is best done through astute time management and the sculpting of your day. Keep adjusting until you find it. Once you find your rhythm, life becomes far less tiring.
4. Deliberately pay attention to how you invest your time.
5. Don't waste time screensucking.
6. Reduce gemmelsmerch wherever you can.
7. Delegate what you're bad at. Become effectively inter-dependent.
8. Slow down. Stop and think.
9. Don't fraz. Learn what effective multitasking means.
10. Play.

Another helpful set of principles that overlap somewhat with the ten above is easy to remember because each one begins with the letter *c*. Since it is C-state we seek, consider these c's:

1. **Connect:** By connecting with the people and projects that matter most to you, you create an emotional atmosphere at home, at work, and wherever else you go. Connecting with others is also the best way to reduce worry. It is fine to worry, just try never to worry alone.
2. **Control:** Control your technology—cell phone, e-mail, and the like—don't let it control you. Develop a system that works for you—when you take calls, how you prioritize e-mails, and so on.
3. **Cancel:** People—and organizations—add activities, but they rarely subtract. It may seem difficult at first, but if you get in the habit of canceling what doesn't really matter, you'll be

amazed at how much better you feel and how much more energy you have. Try to think of at least one activity, meeting, or event you can cancel right now. Pare down your life to its best.

4. **Create:** Create structures and systems in your life that help you get organized. This might mean a new filing system, or a personal assistant you hire for five hours a week to do errands, or a part of an evening you set aside solely for conversation with your spouse, or a time you book into your schedule for exercise.

5. **Care:** Decide what you care most about. You do not have time for everything you care about, so you must prioritize. If you don't do this consciously, you will do it unconsciously simply because what you care about exceeds the time you have to devote to each item on your list.

6. **Cultivate:** Cultivate your lilies and discard your leeches. To do this you must take what the people in AA call a fearless inventory, but in this case it is not of yourself but of your life. What do you want to do more of? What do you want to do less of? Figure that out, then do it.

29 Improve Your Ability to Pay Attention

Attention is as complex as the weather, influenced by many factors, but it's much easier to change. Far from being an on/off state, in an average day your attention goes through as many gradations as white does on its way to black and back. But with work, you can learn to keep attention where you want it most of the time.

Genetics influence attention, but you can't control that part. However, you can influence, if not control, most of the other factors. Here are some steps you can take to improve your ability to pay attention:

- **Get enough sleep.** The desired amount is the amount it takes to wake up without an alarm clock. For most adults this is in the neighborhood of eight hours. We live in a sleep-deprived nation.
- **Watch what you eat.** Hold, but don't eliminate, the carbs! Try to eat in what Barry Sears calls "the Zone," balancing carbs, protein, and fat so that your insulin does not yo-yo all day, causing your blood glucose, the fuel your brain uses,

also to yo-yo all day, in turn causing your brain's ability to pay attention to yo-yo all day. If you have the typical American breakfast, carbohydrates and caffeine, your blood glucose will spike, then dip around 10:00 a.m., and your attention will fade. Try to include some protein, like eggs, bacon, smoked salmon, or powdered protein you put in a shake or smoothie with fruit.

· **Exercise.** How many times have you heard that? Are you one of the people who says, "Every time I get the urge to exercise, I lie down until the feeling passes"? Give exercise one more chance. Do some activity you like, maybe with a partner. *Regular physical exercise is good for you in every possible way.* It is especially good for your brain, improving attention and mood and reducing anxiety and worry. You can also use a quick burst of physical exercise to regain attention if you are starting to space out. For example, if you are sitting at your desk and becoming less and less focused, don't start screensucking. Instead, stand up and do twenty-five jumping jacks or some other quick burst of exercise. It is like pushing the reset button on your brain. It truly works wonders.

· **Reduce gemmelsmerch,** or the "distractibility quotient" in your environment. What makes for gemmelsmerch varies from person to person. Try to detect the factors that influence you, and eliminate or reduce them. For example, if your open door leads to distracting interruptions, close it and put a sign on it reading WORKING. AVAILABLE AT 3, or some such note. Or perhaps a plant would change the ambience in such a way that you could focus on work better. Music helps some people, hinders others. Knowing how long you are going to give a certain task helps many people focus. Deadlines can reduce distraction, but be careful of using this one often. Essentially you are using adrenaline, nature's own Ritalin, to help you get focused at the last minute.

- **Balance structure and novelty.** Too much structure and you will get bored, thus losing attention. Too much novelty and you will become confused or overstimulated, thus losing track of what's going on. You should try to organize what you are working on well enough that you can be logical and make progress, but not allow it to become rote.

- **Organize just enough.** Keep whatever environment you are in well enough organized so that disorganization does not distract you. That doesn't mean you have to be a neat freak or even all that well organized. The danger sign is when you come into your office and feel distraught at what you see. The piles, the papers strewn here and there, the Post-its everywhere, the bundle you were supposed to bring home a week ago, the picture on the wall hanging crooked, all hit you hard and put you in a bad mood. Now it is hard to focus your attention constructively. So take organization seriously enough to keep disorganization from becoming a problem. I look at it like caring for my teeth: Do enough to stave off root canals.

- **Do what you want to do,** as much as possible. Motivation focuses the mind. Doing a task well increases motivation because it is human nature to like to do more of what you do well. (It works the other way, too. A person tends to avoid doing what she doesn't do well.) A logical progression is this: 1) Do what interests you. 2) Being interested, you will want to do it often. 3) Doing it often will lead you to get better at it. 4) Getting better at it will lead you to be motivated to do

it more and get even better. 5) Being motivated will enhance your ability to pay attention.

- **Build variety into your career.** If you do the same job over and
over again, even if you like doing it, sooner or later you will
get bored and your mind will wander. Try to organize your
work so that variety spices your life. For example, I have essentially three careers: writer, speaker, and psychiatrist. If I
did any one full-time, I would get tired of it. But by dividing
my time equally among them, I rarely get bored with any of
them.

- **Vary individual tasks** as well. Just as variety helps at the macro
level, it helps at the micro level, too. For example, try not to
stay in one mental mode too long. Go from reading to writing to speaking. Go from number-based work to word-based
work. Go from meeting with an aggressive, hyped-up person
to a reflective, quiet one. Of course, you can't control this all
that much, but the more you can vary the mental mode
you're in, the more likely it is you will be fresh.

- **Have a human moment** (see chapter 16 for definition) a few
times a day if you can. Speaking to a live human being helps
clear the mind of cobwebs. Just make sure you like the person you have the human moment with.

- **Don't expect your attention to last indefinitely.** Some people run their brains as if they had an infinite capacity to be
attentive. When their attention starts to falter, they think a
cup of coffee or simply more effort will solve the problem.
Not so. You will do much better if you replenish your attention regularly, using some of these techniques or techniques
you make up on your own.

- **Engage your frontal lobes.** If you are stuck in a negative
emotional pothole and this negative state is sapping your

attention, as negative emotions usually do, try tricking your limbic system by engaging your frontal lobes. The limbic system is your emotional regulator. Your frontal lobes are your centers for higher thinking, like planning, choosing, and cogitating. The limbic system usually rules, but you can trick it by engaging your frontal lobes in a simple task, like writing a memo that has little complex content. Your limbic system will likely allow you to do this. Then, as your frontal lobes engage, you will take back the neurons the limbic system had diverted to itself in the service of negative emotion. Once your cerebral cortex (frontal lobes and the rest of the top layer of the brain) has taken back those neurons, you will be able to engage in more complex thinking without interference from the limbic system. Essentially, you will have outsmarted your bad mood. This is analogous to diverting an angry child's attention to some game or treat. Soon he forgets that he was angry or what he was angry about, and he can pay attention to more useful activities than just being angry.

- **Avoid excessive use of alcohol.**
- **Stay away from other drugs of abuse completely.**
- **Take omega-3 fatty acid supplements.** It may be that omega-3 fatty acid supplements, as found in fish oil, improve attention. They are certainly good for general health. Same with vitamin B complex.
- **Promote joy and laughter.** Do all that you can to create a positive emotional atmosphere in your environment.
- **Try mental exercises** to improve attention (see examples that follow).

Test and Train Your Attention

In diagnosing ADD, I have learned many tests of attention. One of the best is simply to ask, "Do you have trouble paying attention?" Or, "Does loss of mental focus keep you from reaching your goals in life?" Simple, straightforward questions, which constitute the oldest, best "test" in all of medicine—namely, the patient's history—reveal more than any other single test can do.

However, the history is flawed, because people are not accurate self-observers. They often do not know it when they space out. They are not aware of how much they miss while they are missing it because they're missing that they're missing it. So it's good to have other tests of attention as a means of getting some objective assessment.

However, these tests are flawed as well. That's because three of the best ways to induce a person to pay attention are to put him or her in a situation that is highly structured and full of novelty and stimulation, one in which the person feels motivated to do well. A great teacher, manager, or coach knows this instinctively. Too much structure and the class gets boring. Too much novelty and the class gets confusing. So the great teacher always balances the two. Motivation naturally follows as the student starts to master the material. We like to do more of what we are doing well. On the other hand, we want to avoid what we can't do well. That's why mastery is a great motivator and frustration a demotivator.

The tests of attention we professionals give to our patients are highly structured. They are given one-on-one, the tester and the patient being the only people present, and the questions are asked and answered verbally. That is maximum structure.

Furthermore, the tests are full of novelty—puzzles, games,

mazes, challenging sequences to keep track of, flashing lights, and so forth.

Finally, the person taking the test is usually motivated; he or she wants to beat the test.

Acknowledging the limitations of testing attention, I offer the following test. Take a pen or a pencil. The object is to point to each number from 1 to 25 in sequence on the grids on pages 186 to 190, and touch each number with the tip of your pen or pencil (use the nonwriting end if you don't want to leave a mark). Time yourself. You'll need a watch or clock with a second hand.

Do the first one as fast as you can. Once you have done it, turn the page and try the test again with a new set of numbers. Your time should improve. Try it a third time. Your time may well improve again. You can see as you proceed that it is possible to train your attention, just as you can train your muscles.

After you have used all five of these grids, you can easily make up others on your own. You can use them as "attention calisthenics" to get you going at the start of the day or just as a mental pick-me-up later on.

They were developed by experts on physical training in Russia, where they have a great tradition of emphasizing the mental contributions to physical well-being.

These exercises, and the ones in the next section, are based on games given to me by Simon Zaltsman, a physical trainer I have been working with since the spring of 2004. Simon grew up in Russia, where he became a world-class athlete, then he immigrated to the United States as an adult. As a trainer, he stresses that the most significant limits we have are the mental limits we impose on ourselves. If I ever tell him that I can't do a certain exercise, he smiles and says in his rich Russian accent, "Do it. You can. You'll see." If I persist, I always end up being able to do the exercise.

Simon stresses mental training as part of the physical regimen he puts his students through. Often, at the end of a strenuous set of exercises, he will unexpectedly add a dozen more repetitions, just when I am panting and looking forward to a rest. In frustration, when I gasp and ask why more, he replies, "I do this because you never know when you will have to call upon your emergency reserve. You want to have it ready when you need it. So you must train to have extra energy so you can overcome the unexpected."

Mental training ought to be a part of everyone's life.

Simon looks like a barge standing on end. His chest is as thick as the Great Wall of China. Over sixty years old, this man who survived a near fatal car accident "because I was mentally prepared" is as kindhearted as he is tough. He teaches children swimming, he teaches adults the science of self-care, and above all he teaches all his students that a person can go further than he believes he can if he will but try.

GRID #1				
9	11	1	19	25
6	10	7	14	2
22	4	13	23	12
5	15	18	8	16
17	20	3	24	21

TIME _____

GRID #2

1	19	7	12	24
16	2	10	18	3
15	9	21	25	8
5	13	23	6	11
14	17	20	4	22

TIME _____

GRID #3				
5	17	20	1	8
7	19	24	2	23
6	13	4	12	21
14	22	3	15	18
25	9	11	16	10

TIME _____

GRID #4

22	12	9	15	24
1	25	19	2	11
21	16	20	7	18
4	23	14	6	10
8	13	5	17	3

TIME _____

GRID #5				
2	17	6	24	9
20	11	3	14	21
22	7	19	4	23
1	5	25	12	8
10	13	15	16	18

TIME _____

Additional Brain Exercises
That Improve Focus and Concentration

Exercising your brain keeps it young and fit as much as exercising your body does. Many studies have shown that what applies to muscles also applies to brains: If you don't use it, you lose it.

Of course, you can overdo it, just as you can overdo physical exercise; this leads to exhaustion, either mental or physical. But as a general principle of mental hygiene, stretching your brain every day is an excellent way to stave off the mental ravages of aging.

Mental exercise can be quite specific. Just as physical exercise can target specific muscle groups, mental exercise can target specific mental activities. The following exercises were designed to improve attention and organizational abilities.

The exercises that follow will challenge you. Don't be surprised if you get angry or frustrated, and don't complete them the first time. But, as Simon tells me, you can do them! Just persist.

The exercises especially stimulate your cerebellum, a region at the back of your brain that regulates balance and coordinated movement but that is also richly connected to a part of the brain involved in planning, prioritizing, and paying attention. This indirect route to these centers, via the cerebellum, seems to have an especially beneficial effect, as if creating new wiring or strengthening old.

If you try some or all of the exercises once a day, you should soon find that your attention span is lengthening and your ability to stay on task is growing stronger. Also, the quality of your focus should sharpen.

The following brain exercises help focus one's attention and facilitate concentration on multiple tasks. All movements are carried out as one sits at a table.

a) Position one blank sheet of paper to your right and another one to your left; then, take a pencil in each hand. Draw simultaneously a vertical line on the right sheet, and a circle on the left sheet. Repeat three to five times, alternately changing figures on the right and left sheets.

b) Draw a triangle with one hand and a square with the other.

c) Draw a circle with one hand and a triangle with the other.

d) Draw two circles with one hand and a square with the other.

e) Draw two squares with one hand and a triangle with the other.

f) Draw a triangle with one hand and a square with the other, while tracing a circle on the floor with same-side leg as the other hand.

g) Draw a circle with one hand and a triangle with the other, while tracing a square on the floor with one leg.

h) Draw a triangle with one hand and two squares with the other, while tracing a circle on the floor with one leg.

i) Draw a triangle with one hand, a square with the other, a circle on the floor, and — in addition — do two head nods forward and two backward.

j) Draw a triangle with one hand, a square with the other, a vertical line with same-side leg as the first hand, and a horizontal line with the other leg.

These are extremely difficult, aren't they? But don't despair. Keep Simon's words in mind. "You can do it," he always says to me when he sees I am about to give up. He knows what he is talking about.

Do as many of these as you can do in ten to fifteen minutes. Just as if you were going to the gym, the key is to keep at it. Gradually, you will see results. Your attention will improve, as will your organizational ability and your ability to control your impulses. You may also see marked improvement in your physical coordination.

The next set of exercises also promotes concentration, probably by stimulating the cerebellum, which in turn connects to the frontal lobes, the seat of concentration.

The following movements are carried out in a sitting position, elbows resting on a table, forearms at a right angle to the surface of the table.

a) On the count of "one," the right hand is squeezed into a fist and the left is directed to the right at a right angle to the forearm. On the count of "two," position of both hands is changing: The left is squeezed in a fist, and the right is opened (beside left). Speed of the counting gradually increases. Clearness of movements is the main condition of the exercise's correct execution.

b) Hands are squeezed in a fist; thumbs are unbent, positioned against each other. Rotate thumbs in opposite directions.

c) Hands are squeezed in a fist; thumbs are unbent, established against each other. The thumb of one hand traces a circle; the thumb of the other hand, a triangle.

d) Rotate the right hand, with index and ring fingers of the left hand going down; thumb, middle, and little finger are going up. With each count, one hand revolution is made and the position of fingers varies (down—up).

e) Hands rotate in opposite directions.

Each exercise is executed five to seven times, after which the hand position switches. It is possible to include this sequence as an element in a daily physical workout routine.

30 Combine Work and Play

How do you induce your mind to sing rather than make irritable noise out of all the projects, demands, and details it handles every day? How do you stay on top of it all instead of getting buried, or at least feeling that way? How do you deal with the guilt of not getting everything done while maintaining your enthusiasm for what you really want to do? How do you quell the chaos of F-state and work your way into C-state? To do all this, you have to anticipate the dangers out there and have methods of protecting yourself from them.

As children, we all learned how to avoid many of the dangers of the world, but when we were children the dangers I am describing in this book did not exist. Screensucking, gigaguilt, and the megaloctopus had not yet gained the strength they have in the twenty-first century. Today, the greatest threats to your living a productive, joyful life come not from common thieves, bandits, or even terrorists, but from the uncommon thieves, bandits, and terrorists who would steal your attention, rob you of your time and mental energy, and terrorize you as you attempt to find the right rhythm in your life. If there were a color-coded alert system for these terrorists, the country would perpetually be on code red, highest alert. These thieves never sleep.

You can create your own personal security system to protect yourself, your family, your office, and even your town if others join in. The key to the system lies in how you use your mind and how you allow it to connect with others. Think of your mind as being the most sophisticated instrument you'll ever own, an instrument that you spend years learning how to use. This instrument has more possible uses than you will ever discover; it can create more beauty than you will ever know. You play it every day, and when you let yourself, you discover a new way to use it, or it leads you to create something new for you and for the world.

But just ask yourself, are you using this instrument in the best way possible? You wouldn't hire a brain surgeon to clean toilets, but that's what many people do with their minds every day. They use the brain surgeon part of their mind to do menial tasks. It is perhaps more accurate to say that they waste the part of their brain that could become a brain surgeon in the doing of menial tasks.

Furthermore, you wouldn't hire a concert pianist and then ask her to play "Chopsticks," yet that's what many people ask their minds to play every day. More accurately, they don't allow the part of their mind that wants to learn to play complex and beautiful music the time to practice. Instead they ask it to play "Chopsticks" over and over again or to leave the piano and go clean toilets.

The great irony in this world that has been flattened is that more people than ever have the opportunity to develop their minds in extraordinary ways, but they squander the chance by keeping busy rather than going deep. How do you go deep? You give yourself time to play with your mind, and you take playing with it seriously.

What is a great career but some form of play that someone is willing to pay you to do? When we are at play, we are in the state of mind in which we are most likely to come up with new ideas, improve upon old ones, and generally produce our best work. Play produces creative work. Hard work can produce great play. At their best, work and play weave together inseparably, each supporting the other.

A common definition of work is mental or physical activity that you don't like, and a common definition of play is mental or physical activity that you do like. But a better definition of work would be mental or physical activity that produces something or delivers some service that is of value to others. And a better definition of play might be mental or physical activity that produces pleasure in the doer. At their best, these merge. If we take our play seriously, we can merge it with our work and thereby do better by our brains and our lives.

By play, I don't mean lounging at the beach or doing puzzles or whatever you once did at recess. I mean something much more important than that. By play, I mean any activity in which your brain lights up, any activity in which you get engaged so imaginatively that you lose self-consciousness and become one with the task that you are doing. It is the state Yeats had in mind when he wrote, "O body swayed to music, / O brightening glance, / How can we know the dancer from the dance?"

Of course, day in and day out there are myriad tasks that do not draw you in to such an extent that you lose yourself—like doing laundry or responding to trivial e-mail or getting your car inspected—but it ought to be our goal each day to spend at least some time in that state of heightened engagement I am calling play.

Furthermore, when you are in the right rhythm, the mundane tasks get done without your being bothered by them, because the thinking part of your brain is playing with some idea while you attend to the mundane task.

Simply put, play is whatever you are doing when you say to yourself, "Yes, this is it, this is what I want to be doing," or, "Yes, I've got it, now I'm really on a roll." It is whatever you are doing when you forget what you are doing. When it's done you feel tired, but a good tired, as after a physical workout.

Your mind *can't* be at play all day. A person simply can't maintain that level of focus for eight hours. So you need to vary your routine. Have time for menial tasks, but also make time for uninterrupted play. As you find the best time to do each task, you fall into the right rhythm for your day, your week, your month, your season.

In previous generations, a person could live life the Nike way and just do it. You could start off your day like a mule plowing the fields. You could plow and plow until lunchtime, take a break, then finish up your day with more plowing.

Today, it is more difficult to do that, because we are called upon to use our brains more than ever before. We must organize and act upon more bits of information than it has ever been possible to get in one day. It is as if now the mule must sprint, and no mule can sprint very long.

I have seen people who try to just do it. Some find a rhythm naturally, and they excel, but many others cramp up around 11:00 a.m. They lose their edge. They become less efficient and less creative. They are heading toward F-state. By 2:00 p.m. they are yawning, tired, and cranky. They have lost their spark altogether. They have become tired mules and of not much more use than one.

These people need to plan how they use their brains throughout the day. They need to find time for uninterrupted play, time for menial tasks, time for meetings, time for socializing, and time for breaks—for food, for meditation, for a quick burst of exercise. Active planning and experimentation will lead you to the rhythm that's right for you.

31 How One Man Helps His People Think

Let me give an example of an effective plan to promote play and thought and to avoid F-state while promoting C-state. This example is from the world of business, an arena we most commonly associate with F-state and certainly not an arena we associate with play. How wrong we are. Business at its best *is* play. It is about deep thinking, imaginative thinking, thinking of what no one else has thought of. The people and organizations who can do this are the ones who get rich.

One such man is Howard Jones, a partner in Jones Brothers Investments, or JBI (names have been fictionalized out of respect for privacy, but all else is factual). Howard read my *Harvard Business Review* article entitled "Overloaded Circuits: Why Smart People Underperform," in which I described the damage that can be done by attention deficit trait, or what in this book I am calling the F-state. Howard was so taken by the article that he sent me the following e-mail:

> You have captured and made tangible a brutal battle we
> face every day in our information and stimulation-saturated

business: how to keep our heads clear enough to actually THINK, and not just defensively react. I consider this perhaps our number-one challenge, though our young people seem hardly aware of their predicament.

Upon receiving that e-mail, I asked Howard if I could speak with him in person. He gladly agreed.

Not being a businessperson—not many psychiatrists are—I felt naive speaking with a master in the investment field, a man responsible for overseeing billions of dollars every day. But he immediately informed me that the ideas I was writing about were utterly relevant to his world and the world of business in general.

He told me that the business world was awash in attention deficit trait, or F-state. "Everyone is so busy," he said, using a word that made me smile, "that they're not looking past the next meeting or the next deadline. Shortsighted is an under-statement. They're frantic [another word that made me smile], defensive, leaving the best of their minds at home. People do not think that their bosses want them to think, so they don't. They're too busy to anyway. And the bosses don't think, either, because they're just trying to make the next set of numbers. We are on a collision course with disaster if we don't get smart and use the deeper parts of our minds. Right now, everybody is running around just reacting to the last bit of news. Nobody dares to do anything else." In his words I could see the rush, the gush, the worry, and the blather, a word that Howard him-self would use.

Howard's heroes in business were Warren Buffett and Ed-ward Lampert (the man who spotted what a value Sears was when no one else did and who later took over Kmart). "What makes them special," Howard said, "is just how focused they are, how deep they are into their own mentation. They consciously avoid distractions and overstimulation. Buffett sits alone at his desk without a computer. Lampert takes days out of his office just to *think*."

As he said that, I envisioned Jack on the floor with the clothes in the motel, making his clothesline. Same idea. Different stakes, but same idea. Thinking about what to do with what's out there. Playing.

Howard Jones went on. "I am interested in the philosophy behind how people spend their time. I'll ask the people who work for me, 'What is the essence of your job?' They'll say it is to make money for the client or some vacuous, rehearsed phrase like that. They are playing defense. Not Lampert. He says, 'My job is to think.' You have to marinate, in thought to develop a radically different approach, an ability to make a big bet that is radically different from the majority. You can't be influenced by every tidbit of data that comes along if you are to be able to go the opposite way from the crowd."

Howard was excited now, leaning forward, speaking fast. "When Eddie Lampert was buying up Sears, most gifted investors were doing just the opposite, shorting the stock. But he was able to do it because he had thought a lot about it. And he got away on a regular basis from the supercontagious group-think that we are all a part of in this business.

"I watch other investors," he went on, "and it is lunacy out there, a thinly veiled freneticism that is considered normal." I thought of F-state and the fear that so clogs clear thinking. Howard was soon to pick up on that theme. He continued, "Most investors are always thinking, What can I do to make money *now*? Should I take this call or read this e-mail? This call or e-mail might give me good stock tips. Most of these investors manage money with quarterly liquidity, fearing that if they lose money in one quarter, their clients will leave them. So they feel they have to make money *now*. That's foolish. Do you think Warren Buffett thinks about daily stock quotes? He couldn't care less.

"But in most investors there is a burbling anxiety, a constant fear. They are perpetually reactive. If you ask them for their strategy, they will fill you full of plausible blather that leads to no substantial result. We don't want plausible blather here. We ask our people to get off their computer screens and spend more time thinking. Thinking doesn't mean staring at the wall hoping that something hits you. It means analyzing the five reasons you have for advocating a certain position, then analyzing the lingering doubts you have, then looking for opposing views."

I loved his term *plausible blather*. One of the chief dangers of the information age is that there is so much information, anyone can synthesize plausible blather. Indeed, many people fall into the trap of believing *any* argument that contains data, statistics, and findings from a recent study, while ignoring every argument that doesn't. Given the plenitude of data, statistics, and recent studies, it is easy to go to Google and find some numbers to back you up on just about anything, while the person who has a truly innovative idea may not have any numbers with which to nail down his or her argument. Of course, I am not opposed to supporting an argument with data; I went to fancy schools for many years to learn how to do that. I am simply pointing out how deviously data can create the illusion of truth, which Howard Jones calls plausible blather. And the best of the schools I attended taught me the same thing.

After we spoke, Howard asked me to come to JBI's retreat

and speak to the people who worked for him. The first speaker was to be Edward Lampert, whom Howard knows well enough to call Eddie. I felt excited to be able to present to such an influential audience, but also a bit nervous about following a brilliant investment strategist. "You know, I am a doctor, a psychiatrist, I don't work in that world."

"That's why you have so much to teach us," Howard said. "Your ideas about attention and thinking and what we do with our time are incredibly timely." So I agreed to come, knowing they had a lot to teach me.

It was a hot day at the Ritz-Carlton near Boca Raton, Florida, where I took the podium after Eddie Lampert. Even though there was air-conditioning, the room was still warm. When I give talks I get excited and wave my arms and pace and work up quite a sweat. That day my talk drenched my shirt. It was only twenty-five minutes, followed by questions, but it planted a seed.

"We have jointly effected a small revolution," Howard told me in a follow-up phone call a month later. "Already a number of people are putting signs on their office doors that read, PLEASE DO NOT DISTURB. More people are leaving the office to take a walk in order to organize a thought and get it down right. The rapid-response BlackBerry crowd has cooled down a bit. People are engaged in active debate about how to encourage deep thinking and deep feeling. That last part surprised me and pleased me, that they took to heart your words about the importance of deep feeling, not just deep thought."

He went on to tell me that JBI was sending its twelve top managers on a three-day sabbatical. They could go anywhere they wanted to go in this hemisphere. The only requirements were that they go alone and that they think. They were asked to come up with three to five big-picture questions to bring back with them for discussion. They would be allowed to bring a laptop on their trip, to use only when needed for research, not for screensucking. They could also check in with their families every day as often as they wanted to. They could swim, they could get a massage, they could take showers. Whatever would facilitate thinking, they were encouraged to do.

When they returned, Howard planned to sit down with them and review the questions. He hoped they would be the kinds of questions that require real contemplation and therefore get pushed aside in daily work. "Your remark about how people swivel around in their chair and check e-mail the minute a thought becomes thorny or difficult really hit home. I wanted to give these people a chance to go somewhere where they wouldn't swivel."

Not being a business guy in my daily life, I asked Howard to describe what he meant by "big-picture questions."

"Questions like these," he replied. " 'How dominant can Google become, and why?' Or, 'What would be the ripple effect if there were a meaningful decline in home prices?' Or, 'What would happen if all of a sudden construction began on ten new nuclear power plants?' Or, 'What about the exurban culture? How will that affect business?' Or, 'What will happen if a whole generation can't write with their own hands?' "

He went on. "What I *don't* mean are questions like 'How many units of Barbie will Mattel sell next year?' Instead ask, 'In five years will kids still play with dolls and action figures?'

"The whole point of the trip," Howard explained, "is to expose these people to the experience of thinking deeply and have them fall in love with it and want to do it often. I want them to become insulated from the action-oriented, short-term work and gradually become interested in becoming more original and creative than they give themselves a chance to be now. They don't quite dare believe it, but that's really what I want them to do. That's the only way they'll produce their best work and contribute the most. The rest a robot can do."

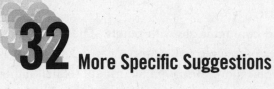

32 More Specific Suggestions

In developing a system that works for you, consider the following suggestions:

1. Whatever system you use, make it part of your reflexes if you can. Habits, routines, and rituals allow you to put your conscious mind in more interesting places than remembering to put coins in the meter. Mere plans don't make a system. Plans often get forgotten or ignored. Plans that become automatic or reflexive become a system. In this book I have outlined steps you can take to develop a *system*, geared to who you are and the life you want to lead, so that life can become somewhat automatic, or what I call "rhythmic," in as many ways as possible, freeing up your cerebral cortex to engage in the important activities it alone can do.

2. Base your system on your knowledge of who you are. Whatever system you set up, it has to mesh with your personality, your idiosyncrasies, your hopes and fears. Don't listen to experts or consultants who tell you there is only one way.

3. Above all, take stock of what matters most to you, and do it.

4. The ten principles outlined in chapter 28 constitute the heart of the method I suggest. Also the six C's.

5. Do your difficult and important work during your morning burst, when you are at your freshest. (If what I call your "morning burst" occurs in the evening, do the hard work then, of course.)

6. Connect and communicate with others. The single most important reason people fail at work or in relationships is poor communication. Bring problems up sooner rather than later. Don't let fear hold you back. The problem will only get worse. Particularly these days, when life goes so fast, it is essential to communicate often and clearly.

7. Say what you mean. Mean what you say. Don't assume a person knows what's on your mind without your telling him. Always ask for clarification when you don't understand. If something is bothering you, bring it up. If you have something to say, say it. Pay attention to the subtleties of communication: tone of voice, body language, choice of words, pauses. Good communication requires your full attention.

8. Listen to feedback from trusted others. Our biggest mistakes are usually obvious to those close to us. If we would but listen to them, or ask for their opinion, we could stay out of a lot of trouble.

9. As much as you possibly can, live *your* life. Don't live a life of trying to please everyone else first and you last. If you have trouble doing this, get a couple of close friends to be your cheerleaders, egging you on to do for yourself, not just do for everyone else.

10. Before you worry too much about what other people think, consider how little they really know about you and how lit-

tle time they probably spend thinking about anyone other than themselves.

11. When you're working on a project, don't gather data forever. So much information is out there that you could research a ten-thousand-word article for a year and not get every known fact, while half of what you found would have become obsolete by the end of the year. Get as much information as you can get your mind around. Then use your imagination to work with what you have and turn it into something new and useful. If you get too much, you'll never be able to assess what you need and what you don't. The information will drown you and your article.

12. Don't try to resolve emotional issues via e-mail. Use e-mail for data transmission, not for topics that are emotionally hefty.

13. Don't spend more time than you must to get good at what you're bad at or don't like.

14. Set a timer next to your computer so you will get off when you need to, if screensucking is a problem.

15. Always keep a notepad or an electronic device with you for putting down ideas that suddenly occur to you. When we think creatively, we usually do so in short bursts. We shape the ideas over long periods. But you want to be ready to capture the new idea when it pops into view. Write it down or you will likely forget it.

16. Keep a space on your desk that's free of papers. Not only will it be useful, it will feel good, making you feel organized, even when you aren't.

17. Break down large tasks into small tasks. This makes even the largest task manageable.

18. Allow enough time to do a good job; don't get in the mind-set

of a bad taxi driver, running red lights just because they're there.

19. Set aside at least a few minutes every day just to think. Even better, a half hour. (This way you might actually do some of your best thinking at work.)

20. Set boundaries around your time instead of just reacting to demands. This will help you establish your rhythm.

21. When it comes to documents and mail, follow the rule of OHIO, only handle it once: Act on it, throw it away, or put it in a labeled file, not a pile.

22. Buy lots of wastebaskets, trash cans, shredders, and barrels.

23. When too many piles arise (and they do in everyone's office), think of them as tooth decay; if you don't take care of them regularly, they can cause pain.

24. Don't feel you must be perfectly organized. Just get *well enough organized* so that disorganization doesn't keep you from reaching your goals.

25. Don't expect perfection. Perfectionism is an obstacle to excellence, not an aid.

26. Don't allow yourself to take on more projects than you can handle; learn to say, "No, not now."

27. If you possibly can, get rid of projects that are festering, going nowhere, and demanding too much of your time.

28. Ask for help. For example, if you have trouble setting priorities or saying no on your own, get help from your manager or a colleague. Also, speak up when you are becoming inefficient. Don't assume that speaking up reflects weakness in you; most likely it is a systemwide problem that your speaking up will help solve. A good analogy is your car. When a red light starts flashing, you don't just keep driving until your car grinds to a halt. So it ought to be with your brain.

When warning signals start flashing, pull over and get assistance.

29. Learn to delegate. Set as your goal becoming *effectively interdependent*, not independent.

30. Get regular physical exercise. This is one of the best things you can do for your mind, not to mention your body.

31. Always watch out for the hijackers of your time, attention, and energy. From bad TV to junk food to get-rich-quick schemes, these thieves are everywhere.

32. Never worry alone. Feeling isolated is dangerous. Make sure you keep up contact with people you trust and like.

33. Preserve and use the human moment. Electronics are great for data transmission, but when it comes to emotion, nothing can match face-to-face conversation.

34. Try to be polite. Incivility is one of the most unpleasant consequences of being too busy. P. M. Forni, a professor of Italian literature at Johns Hopkins University, wrote an excellent book called *Choosing Civility*, in which he makes a persuasive case for the importance of being polite. Indeed, you might use becoming impolite as a measure of when you are too busy.

35. Meditate. There are many methods of meditation, but most come down to this: Sit still in a chair comfortably, feet on floor. Close your eyes. Breathe deeply, all the way to your belly. Focus on your breathing. Let your thoughts pass through your mind without your analyzing or commenting on them. You may imagine a pleasant scene to help you do this or have relaxing music in the background. Numerous studies have proven the health benefits of regular meditation. It also helps reinforce a rhythm in your day.

36. Pay attention to what you eat. What you eat affects mental

functioning and energy, obviously. General principles: Eat a balanced diet high in fiber, fruits, and vegetables and low in red meat and processed foods. Take a multivitamin and an omega-3 fatty acid supplement.

37. Don't let busyness and stress lead you to self-medicate with alcohol or other substances. A couple of glasses of red wine per day are probably good for you. But if you go beyond that often, you ought to try to cut back.

38. If you feel stressed and do not know what to do about it, consider consulting with a psychotherapist. You may fear that it will be a waste of time and money, but if you choose a good one, you will find that it is not. The best way to find a good therapist is to get a referral from someone who had a good experience with the person or to ask your primary care doctor.

39. Take care of yourself. Wear seat belts. Don't smoke. Floss. See your doctor regularly and try to heed his or her advice. Don't get too busy to care for yourself. This may seem obvious, but millions of hardworking, smart people neglect basic issues of self-care. (Next time you are in an airport, notice how many people are obese.)

40. When you feel overload coming on—and most of us can sense it, like an incipient sneeze—try to stop, sit down, close your eyes, and take a few deep breaths. Of course, if you are in traffic or in the midst of a meeting, you can't do this. However, you can try to do it mentally. Just say to yourself, I am reaching overload. It will do me no good to let this feeling escalate. Calm down. Take it easy. I can do only as much as I can do.

41. Give yourself a break. If you lose control, if you bark at someone without good cause, if you suffer a meltdown like

a two-year-old in a supermarket, *it's all right*. Just about everyone has done it. Don't beat up on yourself. However, you might ask yourself why that happened and identify the source: lack of sleep, worry over some issue that's eating at you, recent bad news. Whatever it is, once you become aware of it, it will be easier to do something about it, even if that something is no more than talking to someone else or getting a good night's sleep.

42. Remember the three simple words *I don't know*. In this age of information overload, people often believe they should know more than they do, so they fake it. Big mistake. Just say you don't know.

43. If you have children, spend as much time with them as you possibly can. Quality time really does not substitute for quantity of time, if the quantity of quality time is half an hour a week. Spending time with your children is good for them, and it is good for you. It is time that you will never regret spending.

44. Fill out the Time Value Assessment in chapter 27. Use it as a guide to make better use of your time. (I add this here because I am sure many readers will have skipped filling out the chart, and I want to urge them to reconsider.)

45. Visit a graveyard every now and then, not just for burials and funerals. It is a way to get acquainted with death on your own time. Sound too grim? Then sit on the edge of a field and think, or walk the beach, or look up at the stars at night. It is good to learn not to fear death before you die. I can't see how a person can do this without advance preparation.

46. Don't die without having tried to do what you most want to do.

47. Live from the perspective Rudyard Kipling had when he

advised us "to look at triumph and disaster and treat those two imposters just the same."

48. Don't let technology substitute for thinking. On the other hand, don't think that you can't use the latest technology because you can't understand it. *Just ask for help.* That ought to be the modern mantra. Our future depends upon our becoming effectively interdependent.

49. Remember, you don't plan to have your best ideas. Be ready to catch up when they pop into view.

50. Play. Engage imaginatively with life.

33 What Dyslexia and ADD Can Teach Us About Managing Modern Life

Since modern life resembles the worlds of both ADD and dyslexia, those two conditions have something to tell us about how we live today.

In both ADD and dyslexia, it is difficult to read one line at a time, it is difficult to plan tasks in advance, it is difficult to follow one step after the next. The person with ADD and the person with dyslexia both often resort to novel and unique ways of reading as well as processing information in general. The person with dyslexia may read a book with the book upside down. The person with ADD may read seven books at once, hopping from one to the next, often confusing what's in one with what's in another, but thinking creatively and constructively all the while.

Dyslexia refers to various strange and marvelous habits of mind. Contrary to popular belief, dyslexia includes far more than simply letter reversals. Dyslexic jokes always refer to this one symptom, as in: What does a dyslexic agnostic ponder? He ponders if there really is a dog.

In fact, reversals define only a small piece of dyslexia, or what should be called "the dyslexias," as the condition varies from person to person. Often creative, intuitive, and verbally gifted, dyslexics typically have trouble learning to read and spell their native language. Often intellectually adept, dyslexics sometimes struggle in school and may be dismissed as being stupid or, at best, limited.

For example, consider this dyslexic man's account of his high school years, attending the academically rigorous Phillips Exeter Academy:

> I simply accepted the conventional wisdom of the day—I was a struggling student; therefore, I was stupid.
>
> I was such a poor student, I needed five years to pass the three-year foreign language requirement; and in my fifth year at Exeter—in my second "senior" year—I was taking Math III for the second time (I had already taken Math II twice). I was such a weak student, I passed Latin I with a D- and flunked Latin II; then I switched to Spanish, which I barely survived. . . .
>
> I wasn't diagnosed learning disabled or dyslexic at Exeter; I was just plain stupid. I failed a spelling test and was put in a remedial spelling class; because I couldn't learn how to spell—I *still* can't spell—I was advised to see the school *psychiatrist!* This advice made no sense to me then—it makes no sense to me now—but if you were a poor student at Exeter, you would develop such a lasting sense of inferiority that you'd probably be in need of a psychiatrist one day. . . .
>
> I wish I'd known, when I was a student at Exeter, that there was a word for what made being a student so hard for me; I wish I could have said to my friends that I was dyslexic,

or learning disabled. Instead, I kept quiet, or—to my closest friends—I made bad jokes about how stupid I was.

The man who wrote those words is John Irving. The author of many best-selling and critically acclaimed novels, Irving called himself stupid while in high school and only later showed himself and the world how wrong he was by developing his prodigious literary gifts.

While it can be tragic when students like John Irving are misunderstood in school—most do not recover as triumphantly as Irving did—dyslexics can offer us a clue about getting along in modern life.

This is because we dyslexics, as well as those of us who have ADD, know so much about being overwhelmed. From the first moment we tried to read, we have known how it feels to be lost where others are not. We watched other kids "get it" in reading period in first grade while we decidedly did not. We couldn't make sounds out of letters, we couldn't keep our eyes on the line, we couldn't follow the arrow on the screen or keep track of whatever other visual aid the school used to try to teach reading.

But at the same time, we wanted to learn. We loved the world of stories, images, and ideas. We wanted to get into the world that words opened up, but we lacked the key.

So we made do. Now, thankfully, there are excellent and systematic methods for treating dyslexia. The best book on the subject is *Overcoming Dyslexia* by Sally Shaywitz. But the treatments for dyslexia are not the subject here. The subject here is what dyslexics like me did years ago, back when we were likely to be dismissed as stupid, how we handled the feeling of being overwhelmed—and others can learn from what we did.

Whether we had dyslexia, ADD, or, as in my case, both, we

made do by doing whatever we could. Usually, we did not receive systematic help, because not many people knew of a system that worked. We were just told to try harder.

Left to our own devices, we found our own ways—or we did
not. I remember always wanting to do things differently, and because I went to schools that allowed for that, I did well. I didn't
get to the answer the same way everyone else did, but I did find
a way that worked for me. How I did it I don't know. But it wasn't
the how that mattered. It was the doing it.

Let me make a comparison with my son, Jack, who has
ADD, when he learned to knee-board the summer of 2005. His
uncles and I took him and his siblings out on a boat in the bay
off Provincetown, where we were spending Labor Day weekend.
His uncles had produced an exciting device called a knee-board
and asked my kids if they'd like to give it a try. Of course, they
most certainly did.

A knee-board is, as the name suggests, a board upon which
you kneel as it is towed like water skis behind a boat. The hard
part is getting up from a prone position to the kneeling position
without falling off as the boat gathers speed.

Jack was the first to jump into the water with the board. As
his uncles gave him instructions, he paddled on the board to the
end of the line and grabbed hold. Usually, it takes a person at
least a few tries before he or she is able to get up onto the board,
so we were ready for Jack to fall a few times.

Once he was in place, the boat started to pick up speed. I
could see Jack's face some hundred feet behind the boat. Intent
on what he was doing, he wobbled a bit as the speed increased,
then brought himself full up to his knees and smiled proudly as
he skimmed along the waves, bouncing but not falling.

When the ride ended and he got back in the boat, we all

asked him how he did it. "I don't know," he replied. "I just pulled myself up, I guess." We asked him more questions, but he could not give any specific tips as to how he had handled the board so easily.

This is how it is with those of us who have ADD or dyslexia. We often do better without lengthy instructions. We do best given a chance to improvise, to adjust on the spot, to come up with our own idiosyncratic ways.

In today's world, that kind of thinking can be a great asset, because we don't have the instruction manual written yet for a lot of modern life. The ability to read backward, literally or figuratively, can sometimes decipher the code.

If you insist on minute instructions, you may never allow yourself to innovate. You'll be good at doing what you're told, but not good at coming up with a new way. Instead, you might try thinking like someone who has ADD or dyslexia. Play tennis with your eyes closed. Write an article starting with the last sentence. Write some instructions on how to play a game you've never played. Make up a game. The next time a thought distracts you, go with it instead of bringing yourself back on task. The next time something "inappropriate" pops into your mind, say it (of course, be careful where you are when you do this). Go for a drive and intentionally get lost, then use your instincts (no compass, no global positioner) to find your way back home. The next time someone asks you to do something, consider how you might do it differently. Use the opposite of your preferred hand to eat your next meal. Explain in one sentence how traffic could be made less congested.

These exercises all force you to approach a task from a new angle, or to get to the point quickly without spending much time analyzing, or to rely on parts of your mind you don't usually rely on. All these exercises compel you to "think outside the box," a now hackneyed phrase commonly used by people who neither know what it means nor have ever done it themselves.

But thinking outside the box is second nature to people who have dyslexia or ADD. Our trouble is thinking *inside* the box. It is good to know how to do both. What ADD and dyslexia have to teach the general population is not only how to manage the rush and the gush, but also how to think outside that famous box.

For example, one of the greatest innovators in modern aviation is David Neeleman, CEO of JetBlue Airways. David has major league ADD. He can't remember details, so he surrounds himself with people who can. His knack is coming up with new ideas.

For instance, he invented the electronic ticket. He said to me, "When I thought up that idea, people laughed at me, saying no one would ever go to the airport without a paper ticket. But I went ahead anyway, and it has saved the industry millions of dollars, not to mention passengers all kinds of hassles.

"I think my ADD is a great asset," he said to me. "It gives me an uncanny ability to see into complicated situations and find the simple solution that no one else can see. It is the talent that distinguishes me from others, and I think it is because of how my brain is wired. Disorganization is a small price to pay for being able to think the way I do. I wouldn't trade my ADD for the world."

Of course, if you don't have dyslexia or ADD, you can't go out and get them. These conditions are inborn. However, you can learn from people who have dyslexia or ADD that it can be useful to try to look at every situation from as many angles as possible: upside down, inside out, every which way. And if you can't do it yourself, listen to the people who can. Keep in mind that people used to think the world was flat because their eyes told them that it was, and don't always take what you see at face value. Sometimes a crazy idea changes life for the better: like the idea that people would go to the airport without a paper ticket.

34 The Ultimate Solution

While in this book I offer practical solutions a person can use today to address the problem of being overstretched, over-booked, and about to snap, the ultimate solution is as yet in the making. It awaits the further proliferation and sophistication of our technology, its imaginative application, the recognition of the pressing need for human connections, and the imaginative development of systems that promote them.

Right now, as we all know only too well, electronic communications technology has led most of us to work longer hours rather than shorter, to take on more than we can complete every day, and to be in danger of losing our jobs to outsourcing and offshoring. However, as we gain experience in using the technology, and as the technology itself evolves and improves, it offers the possibility of an entirely new method of solving problems, as well as the reconstruction, in new ways, of what we have lost emotionally and psychologically.

Indeed, the ultimate solution derives from the current problem, extending the very problem we are wrestling with every day even further, to the breaking point. In the title of this book I used the phrase *about to snap*. But what happens when people actually do snap? That's when the ultimate solution will kick in.

Two forces have combined to create the overbooked, busy lives so many of us lead. Each is in a way the mirror image of the other. On the one hand, we are superconnected electronically. For all the advantages this has given us, it has led to many of the stressors outlined in this book. It has allowed us to be super-busy—indeed, compelled us to be so.

On the other hand, as we have superconnected electronically, we have gradually disconnected interpersonally, creating a growing feeling of isolation in the midst of being superbusy, surrounded by people. As one of my patients put it, "People, people everywhere, but not a one I know."

Whether it be not keeping up with friends, not having time for family dinner, being unable to participate in clubs or groups that matter to you, not having time to walk your dog or go to the symphony or a ball game, not having time to discuss problems long enough to understand another person's point of view, the evidence of interpersonal disconnection is as rampant as the evidence of electronic superconnection.

The ultimate solution will be found when these two forces exert their maximum effect. When we feel so disconnected that we overcome whatever it is that holds us back and reestablish community in our lives, when we reach our maximum output and can run no faster and do no more, we will have to learn a different way. I have suggested ways for you to learn it sooner, but everyone will have to learn how to be in charge of technology instead of it being in charge of them; everyone will have to learn a rhythm for their day; everyone will have to learn to do what matters most first; and everyone will have to find ways of connecting face to face to create the positive emotional state requisite for our best lives.

Blogs provide a good, current example of how technology can help us. Imagine having millions of people available 24/7 to work on a problem. That's what a blog provides. A problem could be posted—let's say, since I am a Boston Red Sox fan, how can the Red Sox improve Fenway Park and not have to build a new stadium—and within hours millions of people could offer everything they know, from engineering to geography to economics to history. Of course, crackpots can get in as well. But the instant access to information—and so much more important, the access to what millions of human brains can create out of the information a blog collects—is, well, useful. Far more useful than the uses we have put blogs to so far.

Blogs could become one of the most powerful problem-solving devices ever invented. Through the creative use of blogs, all the talking heads and consultants we've grown so accustomed to could give way to the collective wisdom of millions of thinking heads, all brought forth in seconds.

Let's take one million people, electronically connected. The way most people live their lives now, those one million people race around every day, each trying frantically to take care of him- or herself, wrestling with many of the same problems the others are. Now, let's say these problems could be named and each posted as a blog. Every problem could get the combined brainpower of one million people to solve it.

A blog is just one example of the many potential solutions that technology has already provided or soon will to the problems we now face. The problems of the rush and the gush—excessive speed and information overload—can become solutions once we divide up what needs to be done more effectively, rather than have so many people attending to the same tasks, and develop teamwork to the high art it can be. People working together will not only help solve the problems of rush and gush, they will also solve the problem of worry, which is fundamentally caused by social disconnection. When people feel less alone, when they truly and deeply feel connected to a team, they worry much less and think creatively much more.

Instead of rugged individualism—a trait that has made this country great, to be sure—we need now to tap the Herculean power of interdependence. Leveraging technology so as to take advantage of a million—or a billion—human minds all at once, the combined problem-solving power of all those imaginations will propel us forward like no force ever seen before.

Because everyone can know everything instantly, the world will become more like a small town once again, like the town of Chatham, where I grew up on Cape Cod. Back then, in the 1950s, a telephone operator had to connect by hand every call that was made in the town. Guess who was the best source of gossip in town.

Now, with instant access, it will be more and more difficult to hide. Privacy laws will have to be changed. But, on the positive side, we will start to reconnect interpersonally and develop the feeling of interconnectedness, so sorely lacking today, that will create a better world for our children and for us.

We will connect in the most potent way ever, by stringing our individual brainpower into one gigantic, supercharged, constantly evolving organism, both organic and inorganic, individually accessed but collectively created.

The power of this interdependence will lead to the best solutions. When all of us—or at least millions of people—connect our brainpower, we will solve the problems that seem all but unsolvable today, like global warming, world hunger, terrorism, and the fact of natural disasters.

We will also find ways to re-create human connectedness through whatever the future equivalent of neighborhoods will be. We will find ways to reconnect interpersonally, which is essential both for our health and for the creation of mutual trust.

Right now we are in a period of flux. Speeding up, seemingly out of control, we will solve the problems we face once we put our heads together.

35 Joy Every Day: The Reward of Taking Your Time

The best reason to *take* your time is that this is the only time you'll ever have. You must take it or it will be taken from you. It is telling that the phrase *taking your time* is synonymous with slowing down. If we want to live life fully and get the most out of the short lives we have, we would do best to slow down.

Nowhere in this book have I suggested that we turn back the clock, trying to retrieve a bygone era when life was slower. We couldn't even if we wanted to. But I don't even believe we *should* want to. We should revel in our electronically supercharged, unbounded world. But to make the most out of this new world, to avoid feeling overbooked, overstretched, and about to snap, to make modern life become better than life has ever been, a person must learn how to do what matters most first and to make the most out of each minute that matters.

Otherwise you will bulldoze over life's best moments. You won't notice the little charms that adorn each day, nor will you ever transform the mundane into the extraordinary. The only way to do that is to take your time. Let me close this book by letting an elderly couple illustrate what I mean.

At 7:00 a.m. Morris, called Mo, gets out of bed and shakes the shoulder of his wife, Ruth, called Ruthie. She makes a sound signifying that she is awake, allowing Mo to hoist his aged bones out of bed, find his slippers, and pad his way softly into the bathroom. About twenty minutes later he emerges, shaven and sweet smelling, to find Ruthie and his breakfast of Cheerios where they always are. He loves his routine. Like a kid, he relishes looking at the little o's as they float in the bowl.

Ruthie and Mo eat their cereal, toast, coffee, and orange juice while they glance at the headlines in the paper and talk to each other about what the day has in store for each of them. Ruthie, still in her nightgown, is also wearing a flowered wrapper. She compliments Mo on his aftershave, the same aftershave he has worn for decades, but Ruthie sniffs it as if it were new and tells Mo how fresh and good it smells. She does this every day. Mo would miss it if she didn't, and so would she.

The two get up and go to the bedroom, where, as always, Ruthie helps Mo pick out a tie; he is color-blind and can't pick out his own. From his hundreds of ties, Ruthie selects one, which she says will make him look like a million bucks, "not that you need any help to look like a million bucks, but it is a nice tie." She presents the tie to Mo and chats some more as he carefully ties the four-in-hand knot he has tied for so many years that he could tie it in a coma, a state that he is not all that far from.

Mo is eighty. Ruthie is seventy-eight. They have been married for fifty-six years. Now they live in a retirement home, but Mo still goes to work every day, where he writes insurance for the same company that has employed him for fifty-two years. Mo has Alzheimer's, and it is breaking Ruthie's heart to see his forgetfulness gradually deepen. She dreads the day he will have to stop driving his car and working his job. But she doesn't talk about this. She wants to make every lucid moment count.

Fully decked out for the day, Mo picks up his briefcase. Hand in hand, he and Ruthie walk to the door. Before opening it, Mo puts down his briefcase and takes Ruthie in his arms. He kisses her sensually on her lips and her neck. He caresses her hair and makes soft noises. He tells her that he loves her as he also rubs one breast, then the next, and reaches down and rubs Ruthie's bottom. She makes a high-pitched noise followed by an "Mmmmm," and the two eagerly kiss a bit more, making out like teenage lovers. They do this every morning. They've done it for as long as they can remember.

Mo finally lets go of Ruthie, picks up his briefcase, opens the door, and begins his walk down the long hallway to the elevator. As always, Ruthie stands at the door, watching. Mo, who knows that Ruthie is watching, dances down the hallway like Gene Kelly in *An American in Paris*, turning half-circles, waving his hand over his head, weaving from wall to wall as if he were newly in love.

Once he is in the elevator, Ruthie closes the door and goes over to the front window and opens it. Soon Mo's car appears, coming up from the underground parking lot. As he pulls out, he lowers his car window. Ruthie calls out, "I love you, Mo," to which Mo, as always, replies, "I love you, too, Ruthie," and drives off to work, a broad smile lifting his old, sweet face.

This is what can come of taking your time.

Index

\\\

EDWARD M. HALLOWELL, M.D., was an instructor at Harvard Medical School for twenty years and is now the director of the Hallowell Center for Cognitive and Emotional Health in Sudbury, Massachusetts. He is the co-author of *Driven to Distraction* and *Delivered from Distraction* as well as the author of *The Childhood Roots of Adult Happiness* and *Worry*, among other titles. He lives in Arlington, Massachusetts, with his wife and three children. He welcomes hearing from readers and can be reached through his website, www.DrHallowell.com.

ABOUT THE TYPE

This book was set in Electra, a typeface designed for Linotype by W. A. Dwiggins, the renowned type designer (1880–1956). Electra is a fluid typeface, avoiding the contrasts of thick and thin strokes that are prevalent in most modern typefaces.